To Have Nothing

To Have Nothing

God Bless the Child Who's Got His Own

A MEMOIR

———————

Adel Ben-Harhara

with

Lorna Stuber

———————

Volume One — Ethiopia

Disclaimer

Although I have made every effort to ensure that the information in this book was correct at the time of publication, I do not assume and hereby disclaim any liability to any party for any loss, damage, or disruption caused by errors or omissions, whether such errors or omissions result from negligence, accident, or any other cause.

I have tried to recreate events, locales, and conversations from my memories. To protect privacy, in some instances I have changed the names of individuals and places and some identifying characteristics and details such as dates, physical properties, occupations, and places of residence.

This book is not to be used as a religious, historical, geographical, or political reference text. The information, opinions, and details about religion, history, politics, and geography presented in this book are included for the purpose of enhancing my story only, not to teach.

The terms "South Arabian," "Arabian Peninsula," "Arabs," "Arabians," and "Arabic" are strictly referring to Yemenis and the country of Yemen only.

The term "Yemen" refers to the country after the unification of North and South Yemen in 1990.

Dedication

To my daughters, *Lina* and *Summer*, for giving me a reason to live.

To the six mothers who raised me: *Weinishet, Rukia, Emebet, Maryam, Zeinab,* and *Fatuma*. And the American mother who "adopted" me, *Norma*.

To my father figure, *Ahmed Bansser*.

To the men who assisted me during my childhood days: *Salem Bagarsh* and *Mamecha Mandefro*.

Preface

Since childhood, I knew something was different about my circumstances. I wanted to keep a record of my experiences, so I started writing my journals at the age of eleven, but I didn't have the conviction to say, "I have a story to tell." Recently, though, when I decided to share the twists and turns of my life in a book portraying events that occurred while traversing multiple cultures, languages, religions, and geographical areas, I was confronted with a few hurdles: a language deficiency and suppressed emotions of guilt and fear about my past. Impasse?

Language

I can speak, read, and write three languages, and I have functional skills in two more. When people ask me where I am from or what my native language is, I'm hesitant to respond because the answer is not straightforward. If I say I am Yemeni and speak Arabic, people assume I am a typical Arab, which I am not. But to say I am Ethiopian and speak Amharic also does not present the full picture of who I am.

It could be said that Arabic is my native tongue because that is the first language I learned, but in my first five years, I also learned Amharic and Oromo, two of Ethiopia's eighty-eight languages. In addition, my father started to teach me some English words when I was a toddler, and as a student I started to officially learn English. In the 1970s, when I was growing up, once children in Ethiopia reached grade seven, all subjects were taught in English.

In my formal Amharic lessons, my instructor also taught me Ge'ez. Probably the easiest way to explain the relationship between Ge'ez and Amharic is this: Ge'ez is to Amharic as Latin is to Italian. It is the root language of Amharic, but it is also a dead language—one that is not used any longer other than for formal biblical studies, much like Latin is used by the Roman Catholic Church.

For these reasons, I also cannot give a clear answer when asked, "How many languages do you speak?" Four? Five? Maybe four and a half! The fact is, I felt incapable of writing my memoir in any of them.

I have written a plethora of technical reports and articles based on facts and information. In a similar way that most humans respond to the melody of good songs, I appreciate a well-written book because I have always been a voracious reader of multiple genres. Those I have been able to connect with and still remember are books with emotions because emotion is a universal constant, and that's what people connect to.

None of the hurdles I faced deterred me, though. I chose to start writing my memoir. My two daughters, who initially read only Volume One, told me, "Baba, you wrote plenty of information, but you included few emotions." I felt like a news reporter relaying facts rather than sharing the painful story of my past.

I can only write about my life as a memo! Really? Who would want to read that?! I thought. *The facts and figures of my life are easy to tell, but how do I make the events engaging?* I began to ask myself. *How do I turn my story into one that people would want to read? One filled with interesting dialogue, unique characters, and intriguing situations?* I didn't think there were words to express the fear, the anguish, the hopelessness, and the feelings of loss in the mind and heart of an eight-year-old boy who was left alone and homeless! I didn't know where or how to start to write my own memoir in an honest and genuine manner with the appropriate sentiment.

Emotion

My first fifty years were excruciating, particularly my childhood. As a child, teenager, and young adult, I felt like I was in a space shuttle floating in orbit in an unfamiliar atmosphere with limited oxygen in the tank. I had no one for me but me at that moment!

Did I say "moment"? What is a moment, a brief period of time? Well, mine was years long!

Traumatic experiences and unreconciled questions haunt me even today. Until I decided to write these books, I always kept myself occupied with day-to-day affairs as a means of not dealing with my previous ordeals. Avoidance was my main coping mechanism.

But I knew that to get my story out I had to confront my painful past. When my mind began swirling, replaying events, and stirring up emotions from these events, I was frequently overwhelmed and brought to tears. To tell you the truth, when I embarked on writing my memoir, I had nightmares. I didn't want to acknowledge the emotions; the memories still hurt! Every so often, I remained frozen in front of my computer, and my thoughts zoomed out despite all my attempts to focus on writing. Hours would go by without having constructed a single sentence.

Then, I would put a stop to my futile attempts, leave my desk, and go for a run. Over time, and through this repeated cycle, I began to realize—I had been running away *from me* all my life! Running was not only a coping strategy but also a metaphor for how I had failed—for decades—to acknowledge and process my past.

Guilt

I was worried about hurting or upsetting the people who would be characters in my life story (my family and friends). There are details and events in my memoir that are not talked about in my cultures. I was petrified of violating the norms and values I grew up with and crossing the religious boundaries I was taught not to cross. I didn't want to embarrass or shame my family, but I needed to be honest, first and foremost with myself but also with my readers. Despite my trepidation, I felt strongly I needed to make certain political and social comments throughout the books as they pertain to my story.

Elements of my story need to be told. So I have made the effort to present certain touchy and even taboo subjects respectfully to allow readers on all sides to learn about different cultural sides of various personal, social, and political issues.

Fear

For the most part, I have now processed and reconciled a good number of my pains ... at least I think so. But what about writing about *me*, my most intimate and vulnerable moments, and having to look at my own life in the mirror?

Doing so would involve taking a piece of my soul and putting it forward for public consumption. There are details of my life in these books that no one knew about until now (except the people involved). Now the world will know some of the most intimate moments of my life! The notion of sharing my emotions but also my personal history was scary; releasing these emotions and details almost broke me!

I knew that doing these books properly would be an uphill battle. I needed help. So I found the right people to help me tell my story.

Meet my team!

My Team

Lorna Stuber

When I contacted Lorna and inquired about her background, she told me the following about herself:

"By the time I was twenty-five, I had lived on three continents (North and South America as well as Asia) and had made it a goal to check the other three off the list someday. While I'm fluent only in English, I have studied German and Japanese, and whenever I travel somewhere English is not the predominant language, I make a point of picking up a few words and phrases so I can at least express my thanks. I'm a former ESL teacher who is deeply fascinated with linguistics and anything to do with cultural anthropology."

After Lorna and I agreed to work together, she admitted to me that during our initial talks, she was trying hard not to get her heart set on working on this project in case I chose to hire someone else.

To provide her a glimpse of my intent, I shared with her the rough first draft of the manuscript (80,000 words). In response, she said, "When I finished reading the first draft, I was gobsmacked. Your story could be a university course in any number of disciplines: sociology, cultural anthropology, history, Middle Eastern and African studies, linguistics, religion, even women's studies. Everything I am passionate about."

I said to myself, *She will require the least amount of time to orient.*

After having shared with her my guilt, fear, and emotional challenges, I asked Lorna if she could do the heavy lifting of developing the manuscript without altering my voice. I suggested that she probe me—push me—to dig deep within myself and verbally explain to her my feelings about the events of my life so that she could fill in the gaps in my writing. We would need to have multiple conversations to make up for my shortcomings in expressing my thoughts and emotions so that we could prompt readers to bring their own emotions to the book.

She agreed!

She was the first addition to the team, with a few more to come!

Solomon Kedamawi

I had a burning desire for my books to be written in my native languages (Amharic and Arabic). After all, I'm a product of the places where I was born and grew up. People from back home would be able to relate to, be inspired by, and learn something from my story. Due to the extensive education I received in English and having lived more than half of my life in North America, I found myself no longer able to tell my own story in my native languages. The search for Arabic and Amharic language writers was necessitated.

I met Solomon through a mutual friend named Abera Lamma, a well-known writer and poet from Ethiopia and now based in Norway. I learned Solomon was trained as a medical doctor. He had also earned a master's degree in natural and social sciences. As I dug up more, I discovered he spoke French, Italian, Greek, and Hebrew on top of English. Moreover, for the first time in about fifty years, I ran into a person who had actually studied Geʿez!

Arguably, he is one of the best authors, with the combined skills and experience of translating eighteen books from English to Amharic. I was curious as to how he ended up a writer and why in the world a medical professional would want to write.

Despite his being in Ethiopia and the ten-hour time difference, we agreed to talk and see where things went. He listened to me carefully. His silence on the phone made me wonder if my awkward Amharic, with plenty of English sentences, could have confused him. I was wrong! He was simply listening and absorbing what I was explaining to him. He asked for a draft of the manuscript before committing to anything.

In subsequent conversations, I found many parallels between the two of us: he had been born at the same hospital I was born in; he lived in the same neighborhood I had lived in; and as a child, he played soccer with his friends on the same soccer field I did. He was imprisoned for his involvement with the Ethiopian People's Revolutionary Party (EPRP) as I was. He told me the story is no longer mine only, but that of the two of us. He took the initiative to speak to my relatives and other parties who contributed to my early childhood in Ethiopia. There was little I needed to explain to him. Rather, I gave him the freedom to acquire more information to complete the manuscript.

Solomon was born, grew up in, and is still living in Addis Ababa, which exactly what the story needed. He is the face of Addis Ababa!

Nesma Abdalaziz

The Arabic part was the most problematic for me because most good Arabic writers I know do not read English. I also wanted the writer to have at least some exposure to the Yemeni and Hadhrami social fabric. There are twenty-two Arab countries on the planet, and despite many similarities, we also have significant differences on many levels.

After an exhaustive search, I found Nesma. Nesma was a prime candidate for a few reasons. She lives in my neck of the woods (Calgary), which made frequent exchanges easy and enjoyable. Aside from being versed in English and Arabic, she studied literature in both languages in Egypt. Moreover, most Arabic movies and soap operas are in the Egyptian dialect of Arabic. If she accidently went heavy on the Egyptian side of the Arabic, most likely it would be understood by many.

One aspect of Nesma in particular struck me. Perhaps true to many immigrants, she possesses a strong ambition and determination to be successful! She brought an energy that I didn't have!

We needed a second set of eyes for consistency and cultural aspects, regardless. The search continued!

Haifa Al-Maashi

Haifa has a PhD in journalism and is based London, UK. She spent many years studying different languages, subjects, and literature at several universities in various countries. What I learned after a few conversations with her was very interesting: her grandfather was a business partner with my father, and her mother and one of my older sisters were friends while living in Kuwait.

Initially, I was apprehensive she would take offense to my blunt, honest, and clear descriptions of my past encounters, in particular to my negative experiences while living in North Yemen. Contrary to my fears, she encouraged me to tell the truth despite the reactions I may face. She agreed to add a female voice representing Yemeni women, if necessary.

What else could I ask for?

Tracey L. Anderson

While the five of us immersed ourselves in compiling, developing, and retelling my story in three different languages, we knew we needed an additional person who could ensure consistency and correctness in grammar, spelling, and punctuation, as well as appropriate and engaging story flow, structure, tone, and wording. Lorna told me a little about Tracey.

On her website, Tracey states, "I love words and how they work and play together, and this has been the guiding principle of my career. I seek out projects that teach me new things, satisfy my curiosity, and engage my interests in people's stories and in the world around me." That appealed to me, as did more of her words: "If you need written materials that capture your audience and convey your message clearly, but lack the time, skills and/or confidence to create them, let's connect to discuss how I can transform your ideas into words." I thought she spoke to me directly! Because Tracey lived ten years in Abu Dhabi, United Arab Emirates, she is also knowledgeable about Arab culture, so I was eager to talk to her.

Tracey, Lorna, and I connected on a Zoom call, and I immediately knew Tracey was the remaining addition my team needed.

Helping Flowers Grow

I own my story. I lived the life. I have the scars and stars to prove it. But the product you read is also the team's! None of this could have been possible to achieve without their dedication. They didn't do it for money because I didn't have much to give. They thought my story has value for the reader!

I say, "A writer is a person who makes others smell flowers in words," and these individuals have all helped my flowers grow. Therefore, I start my books with gratitude!

Contents

Introduction

*I*n 2010, along with my two daughters, who were twelve and six at the time, I set out to go back to my birthplace of Ethiopia as well as to Yemen,[1] the country of my paternal ancestors. My aim for this trip was to reunite with my biological mother, a couple of stepmothers, additional relatives, and other parties who played a significant role in my early childhood. This trip was to bridge my previous life with my present one. I hoped that reconnecting with the places, family members, and other people who transformed my life during my formative years would help me confront the agonizing moments from those years and offer healing.

I was born in Addis Ababa, Ethiopia, to a Coptic Orthodox Christian mother. My biological mother (Weinishet), one of my stepmothers (Rukia), and an aunt (Emebet, my mother's younger sister) were living in Ethiopia at the time of my birth, and all three took part in raising me in my early childhood.

Although I was born and grew up in Ethiopia, I have always considered myself a citizen of South Yemen. Since the age of fifteen, I have carried a South Yemen passport, as my father was an Arab from Hadhramaut, a region in present-day eastern Yemen. Between 1978 and 1984, I lived in North Yemen, where I finished high school, established a career, and connected to my roots. Having always desired a Western education, I moved to the US for eight years but then had to return to North Yemen due to my finances and student visa reaching their end. After again working in North Yemen for a few years, I got married and then moved to Canada in 1996, settling in Calgary, Alberta, where I have lived for over a quarter century.

Shortly after moving to Canada, I obtained my Canadian citizenship. Canada is now my adopted and chosen home. It is the birthplace of my children and the country where I have lived the longest. It has been a land of opportunity for me and is the nation that has enabled me to achieve most of my dreams. It is also the only country I have lived in that hasn't sent me to jail!

The Rocky Mountains, which are a short drive west of Calgary, play a significant role in my life these days. Hiking, snowshoeing, cross-country skiing, canoeing, and running are some of my greatest passions, and scenic Alberta, as well as easy access to beautiful British Colombia, offer me unlimited opportunities to pursue these passions while exploring trails and mountaintops that never fail to leave me awestruck. The time I spend in nature, enjoying the breathtaking scenery and clearing my head, is an integral part of my coming to terms with my past and working toward defining who I am.

My purpose in writing my memoir is first and foremost to share my life story in hopes that it will entertain, motivate, and inspire others. But my intention extends much farther. I want to raise awareness and provoke deeper thought and personal growth within readers (as the world continues to embrace multiculturalism) and within myself. I will be donating the proceeds of these books to orphanages in Yemen and Ethiopia as a way of paying back to humanity and supporting children who are faced with growing up without parental love and guidance, as I was.

Introduction

Living on three continents has defined the person I am today—a man who has been influenced by and represents a mix of African, Arab, American, and Canadian cultures. I was taught Islam, Judaism, Christianity, Marxism, and Mormonism, and I have both rejected and embraced various elements of each. My spiritual, ideological, philosophical, and cultural views and values comprise a mosaic that represents all that I have experienced, observed, and absorbed during the six decades that I have walked and run on this planet.

Triumph

Because of my mixed ancestry, my varied life experiences, and my education, I can't be put into a box; I can't be defined or claimed by only one culture or country. In fact, when I set out to write my life story, my intent was to write one book and title it *Impossible to Box*. As I delved deeper into my personal history and my family's story, though, I felt I needed to separate the content into three volumes and choose titles appropriate to each volume to streamline and represent the different facets of my life and ancestry.

When one is migrating to different countries and continents, confusion and alienation are unavoidable. It is in those moments of confronting the challenges of living in a new culture that one learns more about themselves than anything else. Despite my life's challenges, people describe me as a positive, cheerful, optimistic man. And I am! It is true that I try to focus on the positive; on my multiple social media accounts I state, "Not because everything is good, but because I choose to focus on the better moments." I also love to laugh! Laughter is indeed great medicine. My sense of humor and ability to laugh at myself are not only great coping

3

strategies, but they have been foundational in establishing and developing meaningful relationships with people of various backgrounds and identities on every continent I have resided. Laughter is a universal language.

I have struggled to overcome immense challenges throughout my life, but I've also experienced great victories. Challenges and triumphs mold a person into who they become, and we all continue to evolve as we keep moving through life, applying what we have learned as new hurdles and dilemmas come our way.

I have presented the first sixty years of my life, as well as family and cultural history, in three volumes. Volume One covers the first sixteen years of my life growing up in Ethiopia. Volume Two portrays two periods of time when I lived in North Yemen, totaling twelve years. Volume Three covers the years I lived in the US before my second stint in North Yemen. Volume Three also includes my current life in Canada, my home since leaving North Yemen for a second time.

Although I have settled in western Canada and am enjoying a fulfilling life, Ethiopia and Yemen are also my homes and will forever be my native lands. They are where many of my family members reside. They are the countries that provided me with numerous learning opportunities that continue to influence my approach to life's challenges and joys. Only in the past ten years have I wandered down the long road of self-exploration to attempt to work through the trauma of my earlier life while fully discovering who I am.

And, as we all are, I am still growing and learning—about the world around me and, most importantly, about myself. It is my hope that my search and my discoveries will inspire, entertain, and motivate you.

About the Title

To Have Nothing is characterized by a peculiarly nostalgic, reflective tone. Nostalgia is triggered by old photographs or objects and the material remains of the past but also by conversation, the topics of the first chapter of this book. It's a longing for longing; it's both retrospective and prospective.

The passage of time is probably the most basic facet of human perception. It's a process through which the beauty of childhood joys and pains remain. Yes, memories may fade. And traumatic memories in particular may be suppressed, but they do not disappear. Nothing will change the passage of time, but I refuse to deny my past because change is possible. Instead, I choose to embrace and refashion my own past through influencing the course of others' lives.

The title of this book, *To Have Nothing*, speaks to the struggles I encountered during most of the first sixteen years of my life. At the age of five, I was thrust from being a well-cared for child with an aristocratic father and two mothers to being homeless and essentially orphaned almost overnight. For a couple years of my childhood, I had no parents, no home, no food, no future, and no hope. I was at the mercy of the Almighty.

I am a faithful and spiritual yet not religious person, but I do believe that because of divine intervention, I was able to rise above my circumstances and create a productive and gratifying life. *God Bless the Child Who's Got His Own,* as the subtitle, has a historical perspective. It is intended to depict my childhood as well as honor one person in particular who played a role in helping me improve my circumstances, although there are many who fit that description.

In Idaho in 1984, university professor Dr. Kathleen Warner, who befriended me and listened to my story, gave me a record single as a Christmas gift: "God Bless the Child" by Billie Holiday. At first, I was confused as to why she was giving me this song; I didn't know the singer, and I had never heard the song before. She explained the lyrics of the song, talking about perseverance and relaying the connection to the biblical reference the song makes ("For to everyone who has will more be given, and he will have an abundance. But from the one who has not, even what he has will be taken away" [Matthew 25:29]). When Kathleen handed me the record, she said, "This is you." Ever since I started writing these books, I've kept coming back to that song—its meaning and its title. I feel it perfectly encapsulates my life.

Therefore, my subtitle, "God Bless the Child Who's Got His Own," is more about Kathleen Warner, my connection to her, and her understanding and acknowledgment of my life story than it is about any religious context.

Major Life Events

Volume One

1962   Born in Addis Ababa, Ethiopia.
1964   Separated from my mother and started to live with my stepmother and father.
1967   My father died of cirrhosis.
1967   Began studying Judaism and Islam.
1970   My uncle squandered my father's estate and disappeared. Abandoned. Left for two years without a home or a parent.
1971   Rescued by and lived with my aunt until 1978.
1972   Attended an evangelical bible school until 1974.
1976   Arrested and detained three times throughout 1976 and 1977 for being a member of a communist party (youth branch).
1978   Moved to North Yemen.

Volume Two[1]

1978   Completed high school in Ta'izz, North Yemen, and then lived in Hodeidah, North Yemen.
1981   Moved to Sana'a, North Yemen, and started to work for US Aid Development Agency (USAID).
1981   Made frequent trips to communist South Yemen over the next three years to visit relatives.
1983   Made the Umrah pilgrimage to Mecca, Saudi Arabia.

1984	Moved to the US to study computer science and engineering.
1992	Returned to Yemen (North and South were united by this time).
1994	Survived the Yemen Civil War.
1995	Married a woman from South Yemen.

Volume Three

1985	Married an American woman to obtain US resident status. Shortly after, detained by the Immigration Naturalization Service (INS) and lost US resident and student status. (Marriage was soon annulled.)
1987	Embroiled in a six-year-long legal quagmire in a quest for political asylum in the US.
1996	Moved to Canada.
1996	My first daughter was born.
2003	My second daughter was born.
2006	Earned an MBA.
2010	Ended a fifteen-year long marriage; reunited with biological mother.
2014	Ran my first marathon, in Calgary followed by twenty-one more since then, including four o of the six majors: Boston, Berlin, Chicago, and London.
2017	Climbed Mount Kilimanjaro.
2020	Visited the hottest and one of the lowest points on the planet: Danakil Depression, Dallol.
2022	Published my first three books: *To Have Nothing*, *Hope in the Sky*, and *My Silver Lining*.

Map

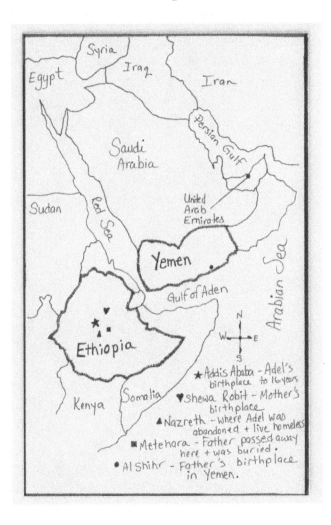

Map created by Janine Shum (2022). Used by permission.

I

In Search of My Early Childhood

*Emotion is 'recognition.' When treasured moments are identified in the
jungle of our personal history during a visual or aural encounter, we
capture magic sparks from our past, arousing flashes of insight and
revealing an inner flare. These instants of recognition may kindle
enthralling emotion and fulfilling inspiration.*

— Erik Pevernagie

The airplane carrying me and my daughters landed in Addis Ababa, the capital city of Ethiopia, on July 11, 2010. The last time I had been in Ethiopia was thirty-two years earlier, on January 13, 1978, when I was sixteen and a Marxist military government was running the country.

As I recall, the atmosphere in 1978 was intense and frightening. The waiting area at the airport on the day of my departure accommodated a variety of foreigners, seated and waiting for their respective flights. At that time, I thought of international travel as something only important people did—those with the means and opportunity to fly out of the country. So sharing the waiting area with those travelers made me feel important ... and taller! Once I embarked on the airplane and found my seat, the flight attendant assisted me in buckling up the seatbelt, as I didn't know how to fasten it. Out of excitement, I hadn't slept at all the night before, so I was exhausted. As a result, during takeoff, I was nauseated and vomited. Luckily, there was a bag within arm's reach for this very purpose.

When my daughters and I disembarked from the plane, I was surprised at how the airport had changed. My recollection of the old airport was of it being much smaller, cleaner, and better organized in 1978. I recalled it smelling fresh and looking bright with lots of light and open space. It was orderly with few people, and most of them were seated, which made it easy to notice any movement from a distance. Back then, it was filled with many more non-Ethiopian than Ethiopian passengers.

This time, however, it looked much bigger and was considerably more crowded and remarkably noisier. In the thirty-two years since I had last been there, the airport had significantly expanded. Now, the pungent smell of chemicals hung in the air, due to the use of cleansers to mop the floors. The passengers were a mix of Africans, locals (Ethiopians), Europeans, and Asians. The airport was buzzing with noise, but it was hard to notice who was making the noise. The air was filled with a sustained din, accentuated by the shouts of airport employees hollering to each other across the hold and on their radio equipment. The blaring of the radios and the shouting made the scene feel as if it were a busy, large, open market. I hadn't grown much taller since leaving in 1978, but this time, I was able to connect at eye level with most of the airline staff. I mused, *Thirty-two years ago, people looked taller and more dapper*, and briefly contemplated whether the change was more within myself than it was in the locals and the surrounding scene.

At the customs and immigration kiosk, the border service officer kept glancing between my face and my passport. It was apparent that to her, the name on the passport and the image of the person standing in front of her seemed a mismatch. My facial appearance bears resemblance to a typical Ethiopian, but my name isn't a local name. My Canadian passport states that I was born in Ethiopia. Therefore, she asked me in English if I spoke Amharic. My response was in Amharic. She then asked as to when I had left Ethiopia last. I replied to her saying, "Over thirty-two years ago, and perhaps long before you were born." She smiled. Our entry to Ethiopia was granted.

Even though I'm used to such reactions in a variety of settings, it reminded me of what Danzy Senna said in her book titled *New People*, "When there is a gap—between your face and your race, between the baby and the mother, between your body and yourself—you are expected, everywhere you go, to explain the gap."[1] In every corner of public places, there is always the need to explain myself.

While collecting our luggage, I started to smell the body odor of the workers who were lingering to assist with passengers' bags. The country of my birth was again, after more than three decades, reaching out to touch all of my senses.

My daughters and I proceeded to the exit, where we were met by the Addis Ababa Hilton shuttle driver. As he drove us to the hotel, my daughters sat quietly in the back seat. I was busy peeping at the left and right sides of the roads to see if I could recognize anything. I could not.

Back in the 1970s, I had thought people in Addis Ababa drove cars with some respect to the traffic rules. This time, though, the situation was chaotic. Everyone appeared to be in a panic.

We spent about forty minutes on the road, not because the distance was far or because there were many cars on the roads. Rather, the roads were too narrow to accommodate the flow of the traffic, so we often had to pull over and wait for other vehicles coming from the front and allow them to pass. Still, I was unable to recognize anything until the hotel shuttle passed by the Jubilee Imperial Palace, near where I attended elementary school.

At one point, my youngest daughter spotted a man who was relieving himself on the side of the road.

"Baba, that man is peeing on the wall!" she exclaimed.

I didn't know how to explain to her why the man was urinating on the wall, so I pretended that I hadn't heard her. Urinating on the streets wasn't something my children were accustomed to seeing in Canada. I, too, was taken by surprise, as it was one of the occurrences that I had completely forgotten are common practice in many countries. I was pleased to notice that the driver sped up and quickly drove us away from the scene.

As soon as we arrived at the hotel, I phoned my half brother Ababe, from my mother's side, to let him know that we were in the city. Ababe is about five years younger than I am and lives in Addis Ababa.

My mother didn't raise me, so while I was living in Ethiopia as a child in the 1960s and 1970s, I didn't grow up with my half siblings. Likewise, due to my extended malingering from the country and the lack of any communication with my maternal relatives after my teenage years, I had no mental images in 2010 of what those family members looked like, so I couldn't even form a picture in my mind of this half brother who was on the other end of the phone call.

The next morning filled in that gap as I got my first in-person glimpse of my half brother. Ababe is about 180 centimeters (five feet eleven inches) tall—much taller than I am. He has a lighter skin color than I do and a dominant forehead. It appeared that his forehead was claiming half of his face! Either he has a huge forehead, or his hairline starts midway back on his head. He wasn't chatty at all, and I immediately felt as though he was measuring me up—observing me and making assumptions simply because I had lived in North Yemen and North America for so long. My instincts proved correct; over the duration of our trip, there were times when he took me shopping for items I neither wanted nor needed, and he arranged for other services that I later found out cost me much more than what I should have paid. I had arrived in Ethiopia excited about reuniting with members of my family and meeting others I had never connected with before, but I was disappointed that Ababe instead seemed to see me as a stereotypical rich North American tourist—one who presented an opportunity for his friends to make money rather than a family member. He was hospitable and helpful during our time in Ethiopia, but his attempts to get money out of me were off-putting and reminded me that although I have deep roots in Ethiopia, my Yemeni blood and the years I have spent living in North America prompt some Ethiopians, and in this case, even a blood relative, to view me as an outsider.

Ababe met us in the hotel lobby that first morning and suggested the order of our visit based on cultural expectations. In Ethiopia, it is customary for a child to visit the paternal parent first regardless of the status of the relationship. However, since my father's relatives are mainly in South Yemen and our flight itinerary took us directly from Toronto to Addis Ababa, visiting my mother's side of the family in Ethiopia was first on the agenda.

"It would be most appropriate for you to first visit your biological mother, followed by your aunt and one of your stepmothers," he advised me. Rukia, one of my three Yemeni stepmothers—the one who raised me for the first five years of my life—was living in Addis Ababa during our visit.

I didn't know which part of the city my mother or the rest of my relatives lived in. Ababe informed me that my mother was residing in an area of the city called Mercato. *Mercato* is an Italian word for marketplace, and this area of Addis Ababa contains the largest open-air market in Africa. I had learned from childhood readings that it was founded by the segregationist colonial power, Italy, which briefly occupied Ethiopia between 1936 and 1941.

As we approached the Mercato area, we saw another man urinating on the street. Both my daughters saw the scene this time and again they asked, "Why do people act that way?"

My half brother, who spoke good English, explained to my daughters, "Urinating in the streets is common in Ethiopia. The government is trying to educate and discourage people from conducting themselves in such a manner, so they have started to build public washrooms."

He added, "Until recently, women were publicly shamed for eating on the streets, but it was acceptable for them to pee on the streets."

I could see from my daughters' facial expressions that this was the most remarkable thing they had ever heard. The conversation went silent for a couple of minutes after that.

Weinishet

My mother was living in a two-bedroom house. I was astounded at how small her place was and how she had managed to raise five children in it. My surprise at the size of her house was perhaps another indication of how much I had forgotten about life in Ethiopia.

When we arrived, my mother invited the four of us inside, and we sat together in the main room with her and her husband. A young girl fetched coffee for us.[2] My stepfather, whom I don't recall meeting in the past, was also sitting in the room. He was studying me; he kept peering at me, up and down, the entire time without uttering a word. After the introductions, my daughters and I were served with a traditional *doro wat* (chicken stew) meal followed by the visit over coffee.[3]

I wanted to ask my mother about my infancy years. My mother, on the other hand, was overly interested in knowing more about my life and my daughters. My mother was a polite, calm, dignified, and measured woman and posed several pointed questions. My daughters also noted how proper and graceful she was despite the economic situation she was living in. I asked her about her health and her children, as most of them were living abroad except for Ababe.

After a few hours, we left her place without having had the opportunity to ask anything about my early days. I didn't want her to think that I had come all the way from Canada only to inquire about my story. Therefore, the first visit ended focusing only on her inquiries. At the conclusion of the visit, Ababe took us back to the hotel.

The following day, I made a phone call and spoke to my mother directly, asking her for a suitable time to visit her again. I also asked if she would join me when I paid a visit to my stepmother Rukia and my aunt Emebet, my mother's younger sister.

At the subsequent meeting with my mother, I pulled out a few pictures from a brown envelope and handed them to her one at a time. I asked her if she had any recollection of those images. The pictures consisted of images taken of me with her when I was two months, six months, one year, and five years old. I also showed her additional pictures of only her, taken when she was fifteen and seventeen. Another of the pictures was of her with the South Yemeni girl she nannied at that time.[4]

She gazed at the pictures one by one with wide smiles and sorrowful looks on her face. There was a long silence. With some amusement, she turned to me and asked me where I had found those photographs. I told her that I had gathered them from my older siblings' and stepmothers' houses in South Yemen.

She told me, "These pictures of you with me and my sister were taken on your first birthday. The others of you at the age of five were also taken on your birthday."[5]

She vividly recalled the times and locations those pictures were taken. She went on with a burst of a laughter to tell me a story about my fifth birthday picture, as I was so curious to learn how human images came to be on paper.

"The cameraman was so taken by you and the way you asked questions. You wanted to see the darkroom and learn how film was developed. He explained to you as much as a child can absorb, as you were consumed about photography. The more he explained, the more you asked. We managed to finally get you to sit and stand still so that we could take pictures and leave, as other people were in line waiting to have their pictures taken."

She paused and then mentioned the photographer had looked her in the eyes and told her, "Good luck with this child … he has lots of questions!"

When I asked her about my birthdays, the day I was born, and her labor when I was delivered, she said, "You were born on Saturday *Tahasas*[6] 28, 1954 at 1:01 am in the Filwoha Hospital (Hot Spring Hospital), in Addis Ababa."

My half brother was busy translating for my daughters what my mother was saying.

Lina, my oldest daughter asked me, "Baba, I thought you were born in 1962?"

I paused for a moment to explain the clock and calendar systems of Ethiopia to my daughters.

The Ethiopian calendar is composed of thirteen months, each with thirty days, plus one month of five or six days depending on whether it is a leap year. There is a gap of seven to eight years between the Ethiopian and Gregorian calendars resulting from an alternative calculation in determining the date of the annunciation. The Catholic Church adjusted its calendar in AD 500, whereas the Ethiopian Orthodox Church did not.[7] The Ethiopian calendar was brought to Ethiopia by missionaries and has more in common with the Coptic

Orthodox calendar, also called the Alexandria calendar, which is used in Egypt. Ethiopia's solar calendar is based on the Egyptian and Julian calendars.

Also, Ethiopia uses the twelve-hour clock system. As opposed to the twenty-four-hour day used in Western countries, the Ethiopian day is made up of two twelve-hour days. The two halves of the day run from dawn to dusk and dusk to dawn. The day starts at 6 a.m. and ends at 6 p.m. (sunrise to sunset); therefore, what everyone else in the world would consider to be 7 a.m. is 1 a.m. for Ethiopians.

Clear as mud? If a tourist has arrived in Ethiopia and set their watch or cell phone according to the local time zone, they need to simply subtract six hours. For example, if a Westerner thinks that it is 9 a.m., it is in fact, 3 a.m. in Ethiopian time since the day starts at dawn. Seven a.m. is considered the first hour of the day. This can be confusing if non-Ethiopians are meeting locals for business or social gatherings. Misunderstandings and miscommunications about meeting times are common.

Therefore, I told my daughters, "If my calculation is correct, I was born on January 6, 1962, at 7:01 a.m. And that is exactly what is shown on my birth certificate." They were satisfied with my long-winded explanation.

They asked, "What is the year and the day today?"

I looked at my half brother for help.

He said "*Hamle*[8] 6, 2002," which was Tuesday, July 13, 2010.

The children thought that was cool.

I asked my mother if she could take me to the hospital where I was born so I could take a couple of pictures.

"Well, son, the issue with that is the hospital was founded by missionaries from abroad, and the staff and nurses at the time of your birth were from India. That hospital was about 200 meters (656 feet) away from the Imperial Jubilee Palace, and as the palace was expanded, they needed the land near the hospital you were born in. They took the land including the existing hospital and incorporated it into the palace property. Then they built a new hospital. It's a bigger facility nearby, about a kilometer (0.6 miles) away from the old hospital."

It would be nearly impossible to get into the palace to take a picture. She wasn't even sure if the original sandstone hospital building was still standing or if it had been demolished or converted into some sort of service home for the palace.

I made her laugh by saying, "Now, I can claim that I was born in the palace!"

After I returned to Canada, I investigated the hospital. It is called Filwoha because of the location; Filwoha is the name of the hot springs near the hospital. But it was also called the Zewditu Hospital and "is named after Empress Zewditu, the cousin and predecessor on the throne of Emperor Haile Selassie. Today, the Zewditu Hospital is operated by the Ministry of Health."[9] The hospital was built by the Seventh-day Adventist Church and was owned and operated by them until it was nationalized in 1976. My mother emphasized to me that being born there was a sign of prestige and privilege.

She continued to tell me about my early years.

"You only breastfed for a month or so, as I didn't have much breast milk. And you also didn't like breast milk, so you grew up on powdered milk."

She also told me that no one would leave me alone for more than five minutes, as I tended to be always putting items into my mouth or breaking them and consistently causing problems.

"For example, when you were a year-and-a-half-old, you saw your father drinking beer and other types of alcohol out of some sort of bottle. When we traveled on camping trips, your father used to carry gasoline to use for cooking on those road trips. People used liquid gas back in the 1950s and 1960s to cook meals on camping trips. Once, there was gasoline in a bottle, and you must have thought that it was your father's drink, and you drank some of it. You had to be hospitalized for several days."

She continued, "Another time, when you were two years old, you found and ate some rat poison and had to be taken to the hospital for your gut to be cleaned. You were also known to stand on a kitchen chair and add salt, sugar, flour— anything you could find—to a meal on the cooking stove. Several maids and nannies were let go because they failed to monitor you. And you used to insert wires into electrical outlets. The expectation was that you might die of some accident before the age of five!"

"Relatively speaking and given the time frame, you were one of the most privileged children. During that time, children didn't have a crib to sleep in, fancy imported shoes, or much clothing to wear. Most never got immunizations or baby food shipped for them from Aden, a city in South Yemen under the British colony. But because of your father's status and wealth, you received all of these items."

"Your father took you to many places because he was so proud that he had a boy. You were consistently by his side. You were five when your father unexpectedly passed away. After his death and when his body was washed for burial services, you tried to wake him up. You wanted to play and speak with him. We had to constantly ban you from the room." [10]

She went on to explain, "There was a significant problem as a result of his death. The Christians in the neighborhood refused to bury your father's body at the Christian cemetery because they said he was a foreigner and a non-Christian man. They didn't believe it was appropriate for him to be buried in the Christian cemetery."

"The Muslims, on the other hand, saw him consuming alcohol, and they never saw him praying at the mosque. He didn't follow Islamic obligations and Arab traditions like fasting during the month of Ramadan, so they didn't think he was Muslim enough to be buried in the Islamic cemetery. That created lots of debates and delays, causing the body to start to decay."

Her mention of the word decay triggered my recollection. I had a faint memory of the smell of his body decaying.

"The mayor of the city had to be involved, as well as the British Embassy, because your father was a citizen of the UK. So finally the authorities decided to bury his body between the two cemeteries."

I have no childhood memories of there being such a hurdle when my father died. Now though, as an adult who understands well the different religious and cultural traditions, expectations, and duties and the importance placed on these practices, I can acknowledge the predicament my family had been in when dealing with my father's body.

I insisted on visiting his grave.

My mother agreed, and after my daughters and I spent three days in Addis Ababa, we traveled with my mother to Metehara, a town 188 kilometers (117 miles) east of the capital. She said she may not remember the exact location of my father's grave, as it had been more than forty years since she was last there, but we planned to ask any elderly folks in the city to point us to the burial location.

When we arrived at Metehara, we found people to help us find the cemeteries, but we discovered the two cemeteries had merged over the years, and we were unable to locate the spot where my father was buried.

I thought to myself, *After all of those fights and the uproar, after all of the religious arguments about my father's burial, it has ended in such a way. Most of those people who were alive at time have been put under the same soil, and now no one is unable to separate the Muslims, Christians, or others. How ironic, and how unnecessary was the dispute all those years ago!*

II

I Had a Family

A healthy stepmother knows that somedays she's a stagehand, somedays she's the leading lady, and somedays she's the audience ... and she plays each role with style and grace.

— Unknown

*M*y father had multiple wives and mistresses in different countries and cities, and of his six children, four were daughters. On my father's side alone, I have three stepmothers and multiple half sisters, nephews, and nieces. My mother had two sisters and one brother.

My mother confirmed that my father was never married to her based on the Islamic or North American definition of marriage, but according to Ethiopian culture, she was. She, my father, and I lived as a family of three for almost two years after I was born. And when I was almost two, my father left my mother and married a Yemeni lady named Rukia. I spent more than three years with Rukia between the ages of a year-and-a-half and five.

As planned, my mother agreed to pay a visit to Rukia with me and my daughters, as Rukia could shed some light on my early years during that period of my life when she was married to my father. Before this trip to Ethiopia, I had learned about her news from my half sister (Rukia's daughter, Muna), whom I have remained in touch with since leaving Ethiopia in 1978.

Rukia

Rukia was Yemeni and Muslim, but she lived in Ethiopia for the last several decades of her life after she married my father. My daughters and I visited her in Addis Ababa in 2010.

My stepmother and I reminisced about old times, and she told me about her other children from a man she married after my father's death. We talked about my half sister Muna as well as Rukia's health, as her health condition wasn't good.

I asked Rukia how my childhood was between the age of a year and half and five, when I was living with her and my father. She told me it was the most difficult time in her life. Apparently, I was a handful.

She explained, laughing, "Looking after you was a nearly impossible task. We couldn't leave you alone for a few seconds without you breaking or destroying various items or doing something that might have caused me a problem with your father!"

She described how I was a hyper boy, and my father was demanding and overprotective of me, his valued son. She found it hard to control me, and she didn't want to upset my father by letting me get myself into trouble.

Rukia vividly remembered and relayed to me a few incidents such as when I put a fork into an electrical outlet and almost electrocuted myself. I thought back to my mother telling me a similar story about my inserting wires into the outlets. It seems I had a fascination with electrical outlets when I was a small boy.

The second accident she recalled occurred when I was riding my tricycle in the neighborhood, not too far from where she and my father lived. There was a freshly dug septic hole and I ended up falling into it, about three meters (nine feet) down. She was devastated, and she was convinced I surely had died. The workers had gone out for lunch, and she was screaming for help to pull me out. A few men heard her screams and came by with a ladder, which they used to climb down and pull me out. She recalled my nose bleeding and my head being banged up.

"I was so scared your father would find out about it when he got home and be furious with me, so I decided to give you a sip of your father's whisky to put you to sleep. When your father came home and asked about you, I simply told him you were sleeping."

Then I asked my stepmother about my relationship with my father and his relationship with her. She talked about the problems I caused all parties. She mentioned that I hardly ate any food, and I was an active child. Just as my biological mother had, Rukia relayed a similar story about how my father was excited about his little boy and took me everywhere. After hearing these stories, it made sense to me as to why most of my father's friends didn't hesitate to acknowledge me as his son when I began to meet them later in my life (including my family in South Yemen, who were well aware of my existence).

She continued, "You didn't cry or complain, but you required consistent supervision. That's what I remember about you."

Then she looked at my head and was amused at what had happened to my hair.

"You had thick, curly hair when you were a child. By the time I finished combing the front end of your hair and moving into the back, the front side already curled up."

Today, I have more hair in my eyebrows and ears than on the top of my head.

As for her relationship with my father, it was tumultuous and rocky, at best. He was simply unfit to be a good Muslim or the Arab husband she was hoping for. The fundamental arguments on a daily basis were because of his drinking habits. He never listened to his doctor's advice, let alone the advice coming from the young wife he had at home. If a man marries a woman because she's shy, timid, and submissive, he has unconsciously chosen a wife who would satisfy his need to dominate. My father never laid a hand on any of his wives, but he did lose his temper with them, as they would all confront him about his drinking and other habits. Just like my father's other wives, Rukia wasn't a pushover, either. When he was drunk, her reaction was to reproach him for his behavior, and that was the worst time to attempt to communicate with him. In fact, it couldn't be done without triggering a family war.

She added, "Living with your father was difficult because I didn't want him to drink alcohol, as it doesn't match our culture and religion, but he didn't listen to me. He was drinking a lot, and he screamed whenever I mentioned his alcohol problem. He was a good man, but the least understood person.[1] Be aware," she said, "that both your biological mother and I were teens when we had children with him. He was many years older than us. He was an ex-military man and was very stubborn."

She looked into my eyes and said, "You are my first son, who I didn't carry in my womb, and I hadn't delivered."

I asked her what she meant, and she elaborated, "I'm not your biological mother, but from the age of one and a half, you grew up by my hands. Your father loved you like no other child in his life. I made sure that he wasn't screaming and yelling at me when something happened to you, and I gave you the care that I have never given to the rest of my children."

I thanked her for the love and affection she provided me when I was a young boy. What I remember about her was that during the three years that she raised me, she didn't speak good Amharic, the Ethiopian official language. At that time, she spoke the Oromo and Arabic languages. Since she didn't speak Amharic well, by the age of five, I was the one who was translating between her and the shopkeepers when we went to a local open market for the daily grocery shopping to buy fresh veggies and meat.

I also remember noticing that she was praying five times a day—one of the differences between Christians and Muslims. And she covered her hair every time we went out in comparison to Ethiopian women, who did not.

As a young child, I used to get quite mystified when I would witness the differences between Muslims' and Christians' daily routines. Those differences never made any sense to me, and I was unable to comprehend why they were necessary.

Rukia continued with the story of my childhood.

"During that time, when you were four years and four days old, I connected you with a local Arab family so that they could teach you how to read and write the Arabic alphabet."

When I was four, before I was old enough to officially start school, she hired a private tutor to start teaching me how to read and write Arabic. She told me that before I knew how to speak and write Amharic, I only spoke Arabic.

"Your father was trying to teach you some English words, too."

My father spoke Arabic, Italian, English, Swahili, and some Amharic. Yes, it seems that from an early age, I was destined to learn multiple languages.

She laughed as she remembered one more detail about my childhood.

"Up until you were almost four years old, you hardly uttered any sentences. You agreed and disagreed by nodding your head."

I asked her if I didn't speak at all.

She replied, "You didn't speak until you were almost four years old. Then, at age four when you started speaking, you constructed perfect sentences in Arabic. And very shortly after that, you spoke Amharic and Oromo. Full sentences without mistakes, adult-like," she said.

Up until that point, she said she had thought I would never be able to speak.

She continued, "What a relief when you finally started to speak! And in complete sentences so quickly! I never heard you talking baby talk. Besides, you were a left-handed boy, and we had to tie your left hand to a chair behind your back so that you didn't use it. As you know, in the Islamic religion, the left hand is used for cleaning. After six months of us tying your left hand to the chair, you gradually switched to using your right hand."

She asked if I continued using my left or right hand. I explained to her that I ended up being semi-ambidextrous. I write with my right hand and shoot a soccer ball with my left foot. My left hand is the first to come up when defending myself.

"You followed instructions and directions very well. But before you started to talk, your inability to speak was a collective challenge. So we let you spend lots of time with Ferdows Munir in hopes that you could learn from her how to speak well." (Ferdows is Rukia's niece who currently lives in Atlanta, US.)

Ferdows's father, Haj Munir, was my father's friend, and her older siblings also knew my father well. Munir ran a transportation business and owned several large busses. In total, he had seventeen children from two different mothers. He and my father married two sisters, which is how the family connection was born and continues to this day.

We bounced between her story, my father's story, and my story during our entire visit.

She explained, "Those days, most children didn't get immunized for chickenpox or any kind of disease, but we took you to the Zewditu Hospital, which was the missionary hospital, to get immunizations. Most children never had to visit the doctor or have regular checkups, but your father made sure that you were looked after when it came to your health and home conditions, and your diet was properly monitored."

"Immunizations and regular checkups weren't thought of. Most children grew up naturally without any issues and without being immunized. Most babies were delivered at home, and many of them died. The ones who survived just ran around and grew up without any issues, so when I consistently took you to get immunizations, one of the neighborhood women was questioning me as to why I was taking my child to the hospital so often. Most of the ladies didn't know I was your stepmother, and I told them you were my son."

When I asked her why my father was so attached to me, she said, "He had four daughters and only one other son. His older son came from South Yemen and attended the Sanford International School Kebena, the British school in Addis Ababa. Your father and his oldest son didn't get along. They fought often and finally, at the age of seventeen, the boy left his father and returned to South Yemen."

My oldest brother, whom I never met in person, left Ethiopia for South Yemen in 1959. He lived in Aden, South Yemen, until Aden was liberated from the British in 1967. Two years later, he left for Saudi Arabia. He died at the age of thirty-nine, leaving four daughters under the age of ten. He passed away while I was living in North Yemen and while I was planning to visit him. Even though he knew I existed, we never met.

"Your father was bitter about it and toward his wives Zeinab, the mother of your oldest brother, and Maryam. He kind of felt he was rewarded with you. He even nicknamed you 'Ade.'"

When I asked her why that nickname, she told me, "Read about it and you will find out."

… Which I did ….

*

The story of my name is more about my father's character than mine. The purpose in my father naming me Ade or Ad was intended to upset Arabs. Even though he was an Arab himself, my father thought of himself as British, and he enjoyed pissing off Arabs who were strongly attached to Arab culture and religion. He often came up with wild antics and ideas to antagonize them.

There are some stories in the Qur'an about a lost Arab tribe called *Āde* (also *Ād or Ādd*), an ancient Arab tribe located in Southern Arabia (tribe members were called the *Ādites*). The people of this tribe were regarded to be one of the original groups of Arabs who rejected the teachings of a monotheistic prophet.[2]

Arabs are passionate about their culture and religion. For example, if someone painted a picture depicting the Prophet Muhammed (peace be upon him)[3] in a derogatory way, fundamental Muslims would be willing and able to kill you. Muslims can tolerate a Christian drinking or committing adultery; however, they are less forgiving one of their own performing such acts. My father drank, and he never fasted or prayed. He was a good example of what not to be when it comes to following Arab protocols based on both religious and cultural values. As a result of his lifestyle, he was consistently subjected to gossip, complaints, and being shunned. He was often annoyed by such treatment, and he was always engaging in a battle of character assassination. A vicious circle, most definitely. He didn't care about all of that throughout his entire life.

When I was enrolled in school in 1967, the Arabs thought there would be a negative stigma attached to my name. Ahmed Bansser, my father's close friend from the same village as my father (Al-Shihr, Hadhramaut, South Yemen) decided to add the letter L to the end of my name. In Arabic, Add is spelled Ade, and adding an L made it Adel. Adel turned out to be an appealing name, as it is used in European, Arab, and Jewish contexts as both a masculine and feminine name.

*

Rukia elaborated on this topic.

"Your father had some issues with some Arab businessmen who ran most of the coffee import and export businesses. They didn't like his non-Islamic and non-Arab characteristics."

"Personality-wise, he was overpowering and commanding like an ex-military person living a Western lifestyle. His behaviors with drinking, going to clubs, and not following religious pillars such as fasting, saying prayers, and attending mosques were frowned upon by the local businessmen."

"He decided to move to a different part of Ethiopia and start a new line of business, so he left me with my parents, packed, and left for the Awash valley to live in a town called Metehara."[4]

She added, "That was the last time I saw you. You were five years old when you left for Metehara with your father, and your father passed away shortly after. From that point, your mother's side of the family didn't know what to do with you. She and her brother decided they wanted to contact any other family members in Yemen to look after you, as my family didn't know if they could handle both you and my daughter, your half sister (Muna). You and I disconnected at that point for about ten years. Then I saw you again for a few hours just before you departed for North Yemen in 1978."

Finally, toward the end of our conversation and our visit, she again looked at my bald head with a side look. She asked me to lean over toward her.

And then she grabbed and touched my head and said to me, "That is so interesting how you become hairless. When you were a child, you had such thick, curly hair."

Today, reflecting my conversations with my biological mother and my stepmother, I would say they were not worried about who I would become tomorrow. Rather, they dedicated their time, effort, and attention to make me feel that I was somebody in the today. Such a notion made me realize that I didn't remember anything that they taught me, but I have rediscovered who they are.

III

How I Came to Be

My origins do not haunt me. Attitudes about my origins do.

— Michelle Paulse

*T*o say my father was a womanizer would be a bit of an understatement. He was officially married six different times that we know of. His wives included women from Ethiopia and South Yemen as well as one who was French. Of these six women, four of them—Zeinab, Maryam, Weinishet, and Rukia—had children.

Marriage and Inheritance

In Ethiopia, the Christian communities recognize three types of marriage. The first two are typically arranged by the bride and groom's parents:

1. *Kal kidan (also called serat or semanya) is a promise or commitment—a marriage by civil contract. Most people choose this type of marriage as it is less binding than a formal, legal agreement. It's similar to a common-law marriage and can be easily dissolved.*

> *Divorce is common with this type of agreement as one partner can simply leave the marriage. If the man disappears, the woman can claim she has been divorced and can then easily remarry. This type of marriage depicts my mother's relationship with my father.*

2. *Qurban marriages are the most prestigious and the most sacred, and they cannot be dissolved. Even if one of the partners dies, the widow or widower may not remarry. A ceremony is performed in church by a priest to formalize the union. Qurban is the least common type of marriage.*

3. *Damoz has the lowest status of the three types of marriage. It is similar to a situation in which a man keeps a mistress on the side; these unions involve an arrangement between a man and a kept woman. It is not necessarily a permanent or even a long relationship. The woman in such a relationship has no rights when it comes to the man's property or finances. She will have no inheritance if something should happen to the man.*

On the other hand, in Islam, men can say three times, "We are divorced," and the couple is then divorced. Although Islam allows women to file for a divorce, none of my father's wives ever did, perhaps due to the potential loss of inheritance. The Qur'an has a remarkable level of detail when it comes to the distribution of inheritance. The system, of course, has been informed by all commandments under Islamic (Sharia) law, so this is not to say that Muslims look at the Qur'an and nothing else, but the depth to which the Qur'an discusses marriage is remarkable.

In Islam, inheritance goes to the deceased's children, spouse, parents, and maybe others. This is not because of love or affection, or because people have returned the deceased's phone calls and maintained a close relationship with them, and so forth. Those who receive an inheritance do so because the Qur'an decrees that they receive the specific portion of the estate that they are entitled to.

The spouse, children, and parents of the deceased are first in line to receive an inheritance. Second in line are extended family members such as grandparents, siblings, grandchildren, uncles, aunts, and so on. The specific relationship to the deceased dictates if and to what extent someone receives part of the estate. For example, "A paternal grandfather inherits only if the father is deceased. A brother inherits only if various other individuals never existed or are no longer with us. Some people replace specific other people."[1]

Those first in line receive two types of inheritance amounts: fixed and variable. The surviving spouse and parents receive fixed amounts, but the variable amounts factor into the scenario when there are multiple heirs. In order for the inheritance to be split fairly, the amounts need to be adjusted somewhat. For example,

> *A surviving husband's share is either 1/4 or 1/2, depending on if there are children. For the wife, it is either 1/8 or 1/4, again, depending on if there are children. Other fixed shares are 1/6 for the father, and 1/6 for the mother. The rest goes to the children, with*

two shares for the son … [and one] share for the daughter.

In some cases, say for example if the children are only girls, and the decedent has no father, it may be possible, but not necessarily always the case, that brothers may inherit.[2]

My Amhara Roots

The two largest ethnic groups in Ethiopia are the Amhara and the Oromo, with the Amhara making up roughly 25 percent of the population. The Amhara, and therefore my ancestors on my mother's side, descended from a group of ancient Semitic conquerors who migrated south and then intermingled with the Indigenous Cushitic peoples of the area. Today, the Amhara are the main cultural group in central and western Ethiopia.

A significant aspect of Amhara culture that remains prevalent in my family, and ironically exists on the Arab side as well, is obsessing over other people's perceptions of one's family and image.[3] A source of minor yet constant conflict between me and my half sisters (who are fully Arab), in particular, is their preoccupation with image and with wanting to make sure that others see her (and me—our whole family, in fact) as being respectable, prestigious, and honorable.

Another aspect of Amhara culture worth mentioning is the emphasis placed on sharing and working collaboratively for the betterment of the whole.

Generosity and kindness are indeed two qualities I greatly value.

Still now, the Amhara make their living off the land, growing a variety of crops, so owning land has always been an important symbol of social status. As in other cultures, the more land a man owns, the greater his wealth and social influence. And Amhara culture is patriarchal, so culture dictates that a couple live near the husband's home after they marry.

Starting in the early 1950s, mass migration from countryside villages to Addis Ababa, the capital city of Ethiopia, became common practice. Migrants were largely seeking a better life and education as life in the countryside was difficult for most, without running water, electricity, schools, health centers, or modern transportation.

When my grandfather on my mother's side died, he left four children behind—a boy and three girls between ten and eighteen years old. They had all been born in a small farming village, Shewa Robit, in the Amhara province in north-central Ethiopia.

Shewa Robit, with an elevation of 1,280 meters (4200 feet) above sea level, has always been a small town.

Based on figures from the Central Statistical Agency, in 2005, Shewa Robit had an estimated total population of 24,886 of whom 13,021 were men and 11,865 were women. The 1994 census reported this town had a total population of 5,360 of whom 2,553 were males and 2,807 were females.[4]

I would say that back during the late 1950s and early 1960s, when my mother's side of the family was living there, the population of Shewa Robit was in the hundreds.

My mother's brother was the oldest, and he was the first to leave their village after my grandfather died. My maternal grandmother and the three girls left shortly after the boy did and met up with him again in the nearest town, Nazreth.

The journey from their small village consisted of walking for miles barefoot, riding a mule part of the way, and taking a bus from the nearest town to get to Nazreth, approximately 300 kilometers (186 miles).

Nazreth, now known officially as Adama, is a city in central Oromia, Ethiopia, about ninety-nine kilometers (sixty-two miles) southeast of Addis Ababa. When the boy and the oldest girl continued to march to the capital from Nazreth, my grandmother and the two youngest daughters—my mother and her younger sister, Emebet, who were thirteen and ten—remained in Nazreth. At the time, Nazreth was a new city with a comfortable climate. In Addis Ababa, land was unoccupiable as it was all either forested or owned by the king. Nazreth was a city of opportunity for newcomers.

My grandmother was a resourceful person and managed to survive by getting along with the local members of the Oromo by bargaining to exchange seeds for salt or milk. She was also able to find part-time employment for her thirteen-year-old daughter with a Yemeni-Hadhrami family.[5]

The Fifteen-Year-Old Nanny's Pregnancy

That thirteen-year-old girl, the third child of the family, is my biological mother. Her name is Weinishet Fertewehal Tachbele. Soon after finding a job as a nanny, she moved to reside at her employer's home in Nazreth, where she looked after the family's young child named Nadia Basherahil.

While attending school and working as a nanny for this Arab family from South Yemen, my mother crossed paths with my father, who was friends with Nadia's father, Basherahil.

My father often spent the winter season in Nazreth, as the weather in Addis Ababa was too cold for him. He enjoyed camping and outdoor life. During the late 1950s and 1960s, he frequently took his friends' children on camping and day trips to Sodere, a spa town about twenty-five kilometers (sixteen miles) south of Nazreth that features lush, shady vegetation.

Since most Arabs didn't want to come with him as often as he wished, he was accompanied by children who enjoyed car rides and outings with him. While most Arabs spent their time hustling and bustling with trades and their shops, he enjoyed his leisure time at those vacation sites.

I played with Ferdows Munir, my stepmother Rukia's niece, and many of her siblings as a child. The Munir children were old enough to remember my father, and they have since shared with me their fond memories of him. According to them, on those camping trips he used to pack as many children as his car would fit and then cooked for and entertained them.

My mother, who was living with the Yemeni-Hadhrami family at the time, often traveled with him to tend to the younger children. During one of those trips, she got pregnant with me at the age of fifteen.

Four months into her pregnancy, and as she was showing, Nadia's mother questioned my mother about her pregnancy. Initially, people assumed that the child my mother was carrying was fathered by Basherahil, the head of the household she worked in. Most Arab merchants in Ethiopia traveled between various parts of the country to procure materials like leather and coffee, or to distribute sugar, textiles, or other items. As a result, the men were constantly on the road and away from home. Upon Basherahil's arrival home at the end of a business trip, his wife confronted him and asked if he had something to do with impregnating the nanny.

After several arguments and Basherahil's swearing over the Qur'an that he was not the culprit, his wife decided to find out more about the situation. After some threats and intimidation, she managed to get the true story from my mother about how she got pregnant. Basherahil's wife didn't believe her husband or my mother, however.

By the time my mother was five months pregnant with me, Basherahil's wife asked him to write a letter to my father and obtain confirmation that the child was my father's. At the time, my father was in Aden, South Yemen. Basherahil stated in his letter that the nanny was found to be pregnant, his wife thought he was the father, and he needed my father's acknowledgment that he was the actual father. Once confirmation was received from my father, the plan was that Basherahil would also notify my maternal grandmother of the situation. In those days, having a baby outside of wedlock was not common and was even more complicated when the mother was an Amhara from a Christian family and the father was an Arab, as was the case with my parents.

My father responded by saying, "Schedule an abortion for her, and I will cover the cost."

His friend wrote back stating that the nanny was five months pregnant, and it was therefore too risky to do an abortion. My father responded instructing his friend to wait for the girl to deliver the baby and notify him of the gender of the child before he would admit or deny that he had impregnated Weinishet. That was not the answer the family was waiting for.

Correspondence and delivery of letters between the two countries took weeks at that time. By the time my father's response arrived, my mother had delivered a baby boy. Basherahil quickly sent a second letter to my father, who was still in Aden, to notify him that the child was a boy.

My father's response was sharp: "Is she a goat, that she delivers babies every six months, or what?"

Another letter was necessary to clarify for my father that the baby was born two months premature. He eventually admitted to being the father of the child and quickly flew back to Addis Ababa with gifts and to embrace the new boy.

As difficult as it was to uncover the truth about who the father of the child was, breaking the pregnancy news to my mother's family was the most challenging and tense aspect of the process. My mother's older brother wanted to kill my father.

Fortunately, my mother gave birth to this baby from an Arab father far from her home village, so the rumors could be kept away from most villagers. The shame and guilt must have been excruciating, though.

*

At the age of sixteen, only a couple of years after she and her mother had been on the move and started a new life, having a child was difficult to deal with. My mother was working as a child laborer, experiencing the unspeakable circumstances of becoming pregnant, and burning in the shame of being an unwed mother. Shortly after I was born, she and my father married (kal kidan) and lived together for almost two years. Then, my father took a young wife from a well-known Yemeni family. His wife, Rukia Atufa, was a devout Muslim woman.

At that time, my mother was single again and was faced with an unbearable decision. My father offered her some cash to leave the house and the city of Nazreth without the child; he wanted to raise his son. She relinquished any claim to me and handed me over to my father. Rukia and my father took me in and raised me.

Considering the hopelessness of her circumstances (and mine), how could my mother choose differently? As a single mother with little agency over her own life and the offer of money to give up her child and disappear (perhaps feeling discarded herself), I believe my mother made the decision she thought would be in the best interest of everyone involved. I imagine she tucked away her mother's heart and surrendered me to my father, a man she probably did not truly know.

My mother's decision to leave me with my father and allow another woman to raise me must have been utterly painful. Now, as an adult, I understand that a mother never leaves or forgets a child. However, as a child, I could only feel abandoned, and this feeling is something I have struggled with my whole life. Children are not emotionally developed enough to have compassion for their parents. Nor can they even fathom the complexities of a mother's circumstances. Children believe in ideals like "love conquers all" and "nothing can defeat a mothers love." As I have matured, I have come to understand mothers and their love, and how they are sometimes faced with the most painful and overwhelming pressure from family, religion, traditions, and the men who have power over their lives. Knowing this allows me to feel compassion for my mother and at the same time wish her situation had been different. The child in me still hurts and wishes she had made a more noble sacrifice and kept me, raised me, loved me. But I know she could not have done so.

While my feelings of abandonment have affected me my whole life, guilt has also haunted her. My deep-rooted feelings of loss have impacted my relationships with women throughout my life just as my mother's regret has affected her relationships with her other children, the children she gave birth to after me. Not only are she and I joined in body and blood but also in trauma, loss, and grief. I grieve for my mother as I grieve for myself.

Teen Mother

Once I embarked on writing my memoir, when I began to speak to my mother about that chapter of her life, I could sense her unwillingness to open up about the situation. In fact, still now, the first words out of her mouth are consistent requests for my forgiveness for giving me up when I was a toddler. However, I know that if she had had the means and the choice, she wouldn't have abandoned me. When we speak of this topic, there is always a long pause followed by tears.

One of her children from a different father once mentioned to me, "Our mother felt like you were her only true child."

He added, "While we, the five children she had after you, are around her, she mentions you and remembers you, as if we don't exist." I can sense his resentment.

However, my mother sums up by saying, "The whole situation was a mistake—getting involved with your father, having a baby as a fifteen-year-old, giving you up. It was something unexpected or unplanned, and the cultural, religious, language, and wide age differences between your father and me made it an almost impossible situation. Moreover, my family was ashamed, and leaving you behind with your father's side of the family was my only option. It was my only way out of a hopeless predicament. In fact, the death of your father perhaps eliminated possible future tensions between his family and mine."

Surely as adult children we still have the ability to heal our mothers, years after we have left their bodies. We could say to our mothers, "I love you because of everything you ever did for me. I love you because you gave me life and gave me the best life you knew how to give. I love you because what has harmed me has also contained the tiniest of blessings. I love you with every cell of my being, and I know you did the best you could."

At the same time, the little child in me still feels the old hurts, longs for his mother, and still asks "why" and "how could you?"

*

Unfortunately, during the evening my mother was in labor with me, my maternal grandmother passed away. Later,

I learned one of my aunt's requests was that I be named *Yenat Fanta*, a reward of a mother who passed away.

It is difficult for me to find information about the events of my grandmother's passing. So many of the people who would have stories to tell are gone. My mother's knowledge about the circumstances of her mother's passing were overshadowed with the shame she felt because of her pregnancy, worry about her future, and her tragic inability to have any control over her own life (and mine). My mother was living at the mercy of the man who employed her and another man who made her pregnant. She likely was not in touch with her own mother because of these circumstances. She may have been unable to properly grieve her mother's passing just as she was unable to properly celebrate my birth.

I know all of this deep in my heart, but still I long to know all the details of my story—the story of my conception, my birth, and my mother's surrender of me. I focus on and struggle with my mother's role in my story and neglect to struggle with my father's faults. This is likely due, in part, to my father being deceased for much of my life. However, I think it speaks to the nature of a child's connection with their mother compared to the one with their father. Moving forward, I have to accept the fractured and heavily censored stories my mother shares with me. She tells me only what she wants me to know and selects the stories based on cultural values/protocols as well as her own desire to keep certain details to herself.

My mother chooses to speak about how my father was generous and kind and how happy he was to have me—a boy.

IV

My Father's Last Years

I should know enough about loss to realize that you never really stop missing someone—you just learn to live around the huge gaping hole of their absence.

— Alyson Noel

*I*n the later days of my father's life, when he was in his early fifties, even though he was already a heavy drinker, the frequency and volume of his alcohol intake continued to increase. He used to get boxes of liquor from the British Embassy and would spend a good portion of the day in the bathtub drinking. He sat in the bathtub because his feet were swelling, and while soaking his feet, he would drink non-stop. He was treated for liver failure and the doctors told him stop drinking, but he ignored their advice.

Excessive drinking was the major contributing factor for my father's death. He always had a bottle of Johnnie Walker or Haig whisky in his car while driving. He was also a chain smoker.

While I don't recall seeing him drunk, I do have memories of him drinking substances other than tea or coffee.

When I asked my mother if she had ever seen him drunk, she said no; she recalled he would go silent and simply go to bed.

During the same time period, my father accidently shot and killed Bahomed, one of his best friends, during a hunting trip. He was held in jail for about a week but was released once the deceased's body arrived at the capital. Upon his release from jail, my father had to pay a substantial amount of money to Bahomed's family as restitution. Bansser, a close friend of my father and the man who would later become a father figure to me, suspected the amount of money my father paid as compensation, and his reckless and lavish lifestyle were the contributing factors for my father's financial, physical, and mental health problems in his later years.

My father was unable to stomach his inevitable downfalls. The drinking continued, and ditto for his deteriorating health, the repercussions of chronic alcohol abuse. I vividly recall seeing him smoking and coughing, and I particularly remember him spitting up blood, which was discharging from his lungs, when he coughed. Perhaps such childhood memories are what prompted me to avoid alcohol altogether.

During the later days of my father's life, his business wasn't doing well. A high public image and great sense of self-prestige were important to him, but his reputation was rapidly deteriorating. He was morally and financially devastated.

One of his other close friends, Baharon, didn't survive a cosmetic operation. Apparently, Baharon wanted to get his nose adjusted, but he experienced complications after the surgery and died. The sudden loss of his friend surely left my father shocked and grief-stricken. Around the same time, Maryam, the wife my father had brought from South Yemen a few years before he met my mother, decided to return to

Hadhramaut in eastern South Yemen with her daughter, Fawzia, in 1958 after living in Ethiopia for five years. Maryam didn't divorce my father; she simply left as she was unable to cope with the cultural differences she faced in Ethiopia, my father's lifestyle, and the climate. Soon after Maryam left, my father's oldest son, Hussein, did the same.

Alone and with his reputation plummeting, my father continued to isolate himself socially, and he became unable to prevent his own undoing. He thought his only option was to leave Addis Ababa and start a new life in Metehara, a small town in the Awash region in central Ethiopia. Although it wasn't clear to most how he picked this place, the assumption is that he didn't like the cold climate of Addis Ababa, as he had continually spent a good portion of the winter season in the more clement Nazreth.

My father purchased family farming land in the Awash area and began the process of building a residential house under my name. In Ethiopia, a person without an Ethiopian nationality through an Ethiopian mother or father cannot own property. Because I was born in Ethiopia, I was eligible for land ownership, so he used my name to buy the land, even though I was only a tot. Of course, he brought with him his British-style habits, which were unfamiliar to the local Indigenous community. (The area is dominated by the Afar and Oromo Muslim tribes.)

Shortly before my father's unexpected death, he had called his distant cousin Mohammed Tahir, a Yemeni man perhaps from his great-great-grandfather's side of the family, to stay at his place in Addis Ababa. The agreement was that Tahir would look after my father's house in exchange for being allowed to use one or two rooms for his own purposes. This man was a conservative Muslim who never appreciated my father's lifestyle. He didn't approve of my existence because the circumstances of my birth fell outside the Islamic rules. Nor did he have any desire to be in close contact with my mother.

I'm sure that Metehara wasn't a destination of choice for my father for his lifestyle. However, he needed to remove himself from the city and the people he knew, as his personal and business relationships were changing drastically. Because of his habits of drinking, eating with forks and knives while seated at a table rather than sitting on the floor and eating with his fingers, and wearing business suits instead of the traditional Arab outfits, the conflicts between him and the Arab merchants were increasing.

A Dutch sugar company was building a large plant in Metehara at the time my father relocated; it was set to open in July 1967. My father died in March 1967. It now makes sense to me that he had moved there looking for a new business opportunity.

My father took with him to Metehara a suitcase of clothing and travel documents. He was going back and forth between Addis Ababa and Metehara when he unexpectedly passed away in Metehara in March 1967 due to cirrhosis.

His death was the start of a new chapter and a series of childhood miseries for me.

*

Later in my life, during conversations with my oldest half sister about my father, I mentioned to her that I wondered where I could be in life if I had had my father's wealth and if he had been alive while I was growing up. Her response was caustic: "The best thing that ever happened to you was the death of your father!"

Perhaps misfortune is life's best classroom.

V

A Drastic Shift

No one ever told me that grief felt so like fear.

— C.S. Lewis

Even now, fifty-five years after his death, I have mixed memories of my father. I remember sleeping with him during my childhood, resting against his arm. And I recall watching how they washed his body and kept it in one of the rooms on the day he died. At that age, I had no concept of death, and I had no feelings about what was happening. As a young child, I simply saw my father's body lying on the floor. I thought he was sleeping, and I wanted to play with him. The other family members had to keep me away from his body and banish me from the room where his body was kept while the dispute about where to bury him was being settled.

Being a child, I had no concept of the magnitude of my father's death. I didn't understand why I suddenly couldn't be with him any longer, and I certainly had no way of predicting how his death would impact my life. With no warning whatsoever, I was suddenly alone. Terrified. Feeling abandoned, and confused as to why my father was suddenly off limits. It was as if I had gotten off the bus every day after school to find my father there waiting for me, but then one day, with no warning and no explanation, no one was there … and so I stood at the bus stop waiting. Looking. Growing increasingly confused and afraid, at a loss as to what to do.

When my father died, Mohammed Tahir, the distant Yemeni-Hadhrami relative who was living in his house in Addis Ababa, was called to Metehara to collect my father's personal belongings. Once the burial service was completed and everyone went off on their own business, Tahir continued to live at my father's place in Addis Ababa. He stole my father's belongings, including his passport and other personal items. Knowing no kin lived nearby, this individual took advantage of my father's death to benefit from it.

At the same time, when my mother and stepmother, Rukia, approached Tahir to ask him to assist them with raising my father's children, he told them he would provide for the children by dividing my father's estate equally amongst all of them, including the children from previous marriages in South Yemen.

Weeks and months passed with no news. After a couple of months, these two ladies—both under the age of twenty-one, with young children and zero means to support themselves and their children—reapproached Tahir.

In Ethiopia, women are discouraged from directly approaching a man for any matter. For them to do so is inappropriate both from cultural and religious perspectives, according to Rukia's views. In addition, my mother wasn't an Arab, so she needed a translator to speak to this man for her. Therefore, all communication my mother and stepmother had with this distant cousin had to be done through an Arab merchant known to my father and the family. Bansser, my father's friend, did a good portion of the negotiations.

Tahir sent a message to my mother indicating he would hand over bank statements, other financial documents, and other assets. At the same time, he wrote to my father's other children in South Yemen stating that the mothers of the children in Ethiopia had taken everything that belonged to their father. He told them there was nothing he could do to assist them. In short, he got rid of both families by lying to them all and found a path out of poverty for himself.

Several Arab families who witnessed the situation begged the man to relinquish any assets or cash he had taken. He refused. According to my mother, her marriage to my father was kal kidan, a civil contract, but Tahir argued that their relationship didn't fit the definition of Islamic marriage; in his mind, they weren't married at all, which meant she wouldn't have been entitled to any inheritance. With that, plus a lack of evidence as to what he took, the court decided the furniture in the house was to be sold in a yard sale, and the money was to be divided amongst my father's children. Of course, the lawyer fees took up a good portion of the proceeds.

While the litigation was on the go and Tahir liquidated everything he could reach, he was diagnosed with brain cancer. As his condition worsened and he became bedridden, he felt guilty and, assuming God would redeem his soul in heaven, contacted my mother about passing on everything he had in his possession.

Accompanied by a couple of my father's friends, including Bansser, the two ladies appeared at my father's house where Tahir had been residing only to be informed by his wife that he had passed away a couple of days prior to their arrival. His wife informed Bansser and my mother that if they ever wanted to inquire about Majid's (my father) money, they should check with her deceased husband at the cemetery. That ended any hope of getting any support to raise the children.

Ironically, and perhaps as fate … or karma, if you will … would have it, ten or so years later, this man's wife transferred the title of the house to her name, and on the day the court approved the title transfer, she died of a heart attack.

Quandary

When I was about five and a half years old, toward the later months of 1967, I overhead a conversation and negotiations between various family members. I vividly recall my uncle (my mother's older brother), my mother, and a third person I don't know were part of this meeting. The discussion was around what to do with me and how to salvage the property my father had purchased in my name in Metehara.

In 2010, I asked my mother about that conversation. Naturally, she was shocked I was even able to recall that meeting. She confirmed the meeting had taken place and provided me additional information.

The property my father had purchased under my name was also lost shortly after my father's death, as my mother had given power of attorney to her brother, who was dishonest. With the power of attorney my mother had granted him, he sold the land that belonged to my father. To this today, no one knows what happened to the money. In 2010, my mother painfully admitted this unfortunate event and asked me to accept her apology.

My uncle also took more than his share by looting the tools and materials my father had bought to complete the house that was under construction on the land. My uncle basically took whatever he was able to put his hands on.

My father had been wealthy. He changed cars every eight months when most people didn't even have disposable income beyond living hand-to-mouth. He had a TV and a fridge, which most people had never even heard of at that time. And because of his service in the British military, he had access to the British Embassy, where goods and services were available to him to purchase or use.

Prior to the brief period of self-destruction in his later years, my father had been a dignified, well-respected man with numerous assets. He tried to be an upstanding man, living his life under British influence rather than following Arab culture. He was a dominant, strong man with a booming voice, and he was a successful businessman—tall, well-mannered, and distinguished.

With his death, though, and the corruption of those who were trusted to look after his children and his affairs, my father's standing in the community and all of his documentation were lost, along with his money and other belongings. Records of his service in British Somaliland, Mombasa, Aden (South Yemen), and Kenya have all vanished. My father's untimely death greatly benefited those who took advantage of the situation. Between my father's distant relatives who had moved into his house in Addis Ababa and my uncle—God knows what he did to the land, house, and other materials he took—my father's entire estate was taken from those entitled to it.

When researching for this book, I approached the children and grandchildren of the Tahir family, who lived and are still living at my father's house in Addis Ababa. I asked for pictures and other items belonging to my father. The family told me their mother had burned all materials belonging to my father.

I can see why these children and grandchildren were not bothered that all my father's records had been destroyed because he was not the typical Muslim and he did not respect their father. Their father was a poor man who raised eleven children on a limited income. He consistently came to my father's house to borrow money or perform bookkeeping work to feed his children. Destroying my father's property and legacy was a chance for revenge with no accountability, so he took over everything that my had father left in the house and ran with it. This man was both jealous of and angry with my father.

Looking back, I don't mind losing all the money or whatever property we were supposed to have, but nothing is as disappointing as losing all the sentimental value of my father's records that were left in that house. Fifty-five years after my father's death, I reached out to the British Government to inquire about and was luckily able to obtain my father's military records and some replicas of his medals.

I am happy now though, not knowing what I lost. I was only five years old at the time of my father's death, so I didn't have any concept of monetary value. I was too young to know what it meant to be wealthy, so I had no understanding of what I lost. Therefore, now when I look back at my childhood, I don't miss what I never had.

Yes, I was told my father was one of the richest men in Addis Ababa. For the first five years of my life, I had had advantages that few other children around me had. It didn't matter though; from that point on I had no place to sleep. I had no food to eat. I was an orphan for all practical purposes because my father had passed away and my mother was not with me. With his death, I was yanked from my life as a privileged, well-cared-for child and became a homeless orphan.

I had no means to reach out to my family in South Yemen, and I had no money to travel to South Yemen to be with them. Nor did I know the way to South Yemen. Had I been older, perhaps I could have had more control over my future, but I was such a young child—I was at the mercy of my older family members.

At that time, there was an Ethiopian businessman who had opened many hotel chains in Ethiopia. According to Bansser and other Arabs, this man, Bekele Mola, used to borrow money from my father to expand his local hotel franchise. When my father's friends (mainly Bansser) approached him to inquire about the loans he had taken from my father, Bekele Mola requested the documents that he had signed and given to my father, which, of course no one was able to access because of Tahir. Therefore, without any proof that he owed money to my father, Bekele Mola was never required to repay the loans.

One day, Bansser took my mother to see Bekele Mola and ask him if he would repay the money he had borrowed so that it could to go Majid's children. He responded, "Sign for me a paper promising that you won't come back again, and I will give you $600." Bansser became angry because he knew Bekele Mola had borrowed a lot more money than he was willing to share. As the principled man he was, Bansser simply said, "If that's what you're offering, forget it. I don't need it," and walked away. That sum of money was huge for its time, but the principle was at stake.

Although Bekele Mola became the most successful entrepreneur in Ethiopia, I recently learned his business ultimately lost its high status. I started to wonder if there is something to this idea of karma after all!

Two years after my father's death, several cargo containers belonging to him were found at the custom clearance yard in Addis Ababa. Apparently, it was a shipment of perishable materials which were found to be unsafe to be used and had to be sent to landfill. In addition, no one wanted to claim it, as there were huge fees on the use of the yard where the merchandise was kept for over two years. Anything the authorities were able to salvage was applied to the cost to dispose of the materials.

My mother had initially entered into an arrangement with my father that he and my stepmother would care for me because as an unwed mother when I was born, my mother was not accepted by her family. She needed to be married and have someone to look after her, so by the time my father died, she had been married for two years and had given birth to another child. Her husband had no interest in having me in his life. He wanted to raise only his own children.

The adults decided that I should be moved to the city of Nazreth at the age of five and half. Ostensibly, in Nazreth, an uncle (my mother's older brother) and a Yemeni-Hadhrami family—the family my mother had worked for as a nanny (the Basherahils)—were willing to share in supporting me until my situation was sorted out with my family in South Yemen. The

Yemeni-Hadhrami family was willing to teach me Arabian customs, pay for Arabic school, and purchase a couple of changes of clothing every year. I wouldn't be living with them, but they would assist in supporting me financially. My uncle had agreed that I would spend most of the evenings at his house, and he would cover my room and board as well as the Amharic school expenses.

So, in 1967, shortly after my father's death, my uncle assumed the responsibility of raising me temporarily in Nazreth. Everyone I saw was new to me, and in my mind, I knew none of these people were related to me. I wasn't scared, but I felt confused and disconnected. No one had had a conversation with me to explain what was happening or to prepare me for a major shift in my life.

In my dreams at that time, which I still vividly recall, I was flying like a bird. I couldn't ground myself—I couldn't get my feet under me and stand up straight. I had been pushed out of the nest. I was soaring aimlessly, not sure where to go, how to get there.

*

Learning what happened to my father's wealth wasn't something I've ever concerned myself with. I did, however find the fate of those who meddled with his money to be fascinating. I have never lived with the idea that karma is a real thing. I must say, humans are not punished for their sins— a sin is a religious violation. Rather, they are punished by the law of nature for their wrongdoing. I would say the natural law is vindictive, and it goes after those who go out of their way to hurt others. Such people will end up broke and alone.

VI

My Education

The Lord God has chosen you to be a people for his treasured possession, out of all the peoples who are on the face of the earth.

— Deuteronomy 7:6

S hortly after I moved to Nazreth, I started to attend Arabic and Amharic schools simultaneously.

Gideon

My Amharic language teacher was from the Dembiya region, near the city of Gondar and by Lake Tana, in northern Ethiopia. Lake Tana, Ethiopia's largest lake, is of great significance as it is the source of the Blue Nile. It was formed about five million years ago due to volcanic activity in the area—what is now an Amhara region in the northwestern Ethiopian Highlands. A dam controls the flow of water into the Blue Nile from Lake Tana, so the depth of the lake fluctuates with the release of water into the Nile and the impact of rainfall.[1]

> *Because of the large seasonal variations in the inflow of*
> *its tributaries, rain, and evaporation, the water levels of*
> *Lake Tana typically vary by 2-2.5 meters (6.6-8.2 feet)*
> *in a year, peaking in September-October just after the*
> *main wet season. When the water levels are high, the*
> *plains around the lake often are flooded and other*
> *permanent swamps in the region become connected to the*
> *lake.[2]*

As is well-known about the Nile, flooding is an essential component for agriculture.

There are several islands in Lake Tana, many of which have monasteries on them, but changes in the water level also determine how many islands are in the lake at any given time. It is believed that the monasteries were built over earlier religious sites including Tana Qirqos, which was "said to have housed the Ark of the Covenant before it was moved to Axum."[3]

These days, the monasteries contain the remains of ancient Ethiopian emperors and treasures of the Ethiopian Church. One of the islands, Tana Qirqos, houses a rock on which the Virgin Mary is said to have rested on her journey back from Egypt. A second island, Tana Cherqos, is where Frumentius, who introduced Christianity to Ethiopia, is allegedly buried.[4] As I began my language lessons, I was also about to begin learning about these significant religious sites and details.

My uncle didn't read or write himself, but he arranged for me to have a private tutor to teach me how to read and write the Amharic language. The person who agreed to teach me was a man in his thirties named Gideon. The first day I was sent to his place to learn Amharic, he asked me about my name.

"My name is Adel," I told him.

"This is not an Amharic name. What is your origin?" he probed me.

"I don't know."

"Well, what's your mother's name?" he grilled me.

"Which one?" I replied.

"A boy can only have one mother," he told me, gruffly.

Gideon was calm and never lost his temper, but he was strict, and he spoke sharply and in short sentences. He always presented his teachings as being superior to others. He was dismissive of the teachings of Christianity and Islam, and he thought both religions were fake. To him, Judaism was the only religion.

I always found him to be carrying resentment, and he rarely smiled. He was keen to convince me that I was from the chosen race and that I was smart and able. He was dedicated to making me one of his best students. Once he knew that I was partially Yemeni, his eagerness to help me the master the language grew. I still recall his scent: like leather parchment. He was an uncompromising man with a sense of purpose.

"And what is your father's name?" he continued.

"His name is Majid, but he is dead."

"Is Majid Ethiopian?" he asked.

I said, "No, he is British."

"Is he white?"

"No."

"But he is an Arab Hadhrami from South Yemen? What is his family name?" he continued with the questions.

"Ben-Harhara."

My first week of the session was all about Gideon inquiring as to my parental background.

I wasn't even six years old when I began to be faced with questions about my ethnicity. Up until that point, I was only able to differentiate people based on physical attributes such as height, complexion/color, build, or gender. I never knew people could also be classified by race. I thought names were used to distinguish items like fork, plate, and knife, not families or ancestry. To me, a mother was someone who looked after a child, not the person who gave birth to the child. Gideon's questions, and the many similar questions that I continue to be asked to this day, didn't make me unsure of myself or feel less of a person; rather, I was perplexed and began to become sensitive to and aware of those differences.

And then he asked me if I was circumcised.

Gideon's People, My People

As part of getting to know each other, Gideon told me he was from northern Ethiopia, and he was from Beta Israel (the House of Israel).

Ethnologists believe that the Jews of Ethiopia from Beta Israel descended from ancient inhabitants of Ethiopia who were members of the Agaw tribes, "Cushitic-speaking people of the northern highlands of Ethiopia."[5] Jews who were already living in Ethiopia, or those from Southern Arabia or upper Egypt, are believed to have converted members of the Agaw tribes to Judaism. One of the theories related to their origins "asserts that they are descendants of the notables of Jerusalem who accompanied to his country Menelik the First, the son of King Solomon and the Queen of Sheba."[6]

My father's people are *Yehuda* (Jewish) people who came from Southern Arabia. All Southern Arabian people were Jewish at one time. Gideon thought that possibly my father's and mother's families descend from the same bloodline. He also thought that his ancestors came from Arabian land, the Himyar Kingdom in South Yemen. In fact, he concluded that my father's side of my family could well be related to him over the centuries.

Gideon happened tohe was have an older brother who studied in Israel, and he asked his brother about my family name. Apparently, my family name means "the son of the hills" in Hebrew.

He told me, "You are related to Menelik the First, who was the son of King Solomon and the Queen of Sheba." He concluded that I was a Jewish descendant. It all made zero sense to me. And I had no idea why I was supposed to care about any of this!

Both Yemen and Ethiopia claim the Queen of Sheba as their own, and her tomb has never been found. Yemen has had multiple queens, and so to the Yemeni, the Queen of Sheba is simply one of many. Ethiopians, however, base their whole existence on her; their identity is tied to King Solomon. The majority of archaeologists believe that she is Yemeni.

Regardless, I am surely connected to her as my roots are both Ethiopian and Yemeni. Now that I understand the history and genealogy, I facetiously but confidently tell people, "If she is Yemeni, she is my auntie! If she is Ethiopian, she is my auntie!"

Gideon told me, "Most of our people refused to accept both Christianity and Islam, and my people were persecuted for centuries."

The thirteenth to sixteenth centuries saw an increase in the persecution of the Jews of Ethiopia by Coptic Christians and European missionaries. Part of the persecution included forced baptism. Those who refused to be baptized were murdered, and among those who fell into this group was King Gideon. Eventually, the Jews were allowed to resume practice of their religion, but by then, many had been forcibly converted to Christianity.[7]

The majority of the Ethiopian Jews lived in their own small villages in northwest Ethiopia near Lake Tana prior to the twentieth century. If they were in villages with other Ethiopians, they lived in their own communities within the village and kept a clear separation from the other cultural group. "In the town of Gondar, for instance, a river separated the two communities, and when the Jews returned from the Christian zone they dipped in the river"[8] to cleanse themselves.

In light of this history of the Ethiopian Jews being persecuted and of forced baptism by the Christians, Gideon's fervor and determination when it came to preserving his religion, its practices, and the Ge'ez language now make complete sense. I suspect his name (perhaps he was named after King Gideon) had something to do with his devotion, as well.

*

In the subsequent weeks, we started with the Amharic language's alphabets. As we progressed into sentence construction, he told me that the Amharic language is written using a slightly modified form of the alphabet that is used for writing the Geʻez language. He informed me that I had to learn Geʻez in order to know Amharic fully.

"I speak the Agaw language, but most of Agaw is related to Geʻez and Amharic," he added.

I asked what the Geʻez language was.

"Geʻez is a Semitic language of the Southern Arabian languages. In the Amharic language, there are thirty-three basic characters, each of which has seven forms, depending on which vowel is to be pronounced in the syllable," he explained.

Scholars refer to Geʻez as Classical Ethiopic, and its origins are in what is now Eritrea and northern Ethiopia in East Africa.

> *Today, Geʻez is used only as the main liturgical language of the Ethiopian Orthodox Tewahedo Church and Eritrean Orthodox Tewahedo Church, the Ethiopian Catholic Church and Eritrean Catholic Church, and the Beta Israel Jewish community.[9]*

After a couple of months, Gideon led me to a large parchment. It was the Holy Bible.

"In our tradition, the Torah[10] remains in a resting position while just the parchment is raised," he explained to me.

I started reading the Holy Bible. He had me read the *Tanakh* (the Hebrew Bible) and the Old Testament, which was comprised of eighty-one books, but he wanted me to read only the first forty-six.[11]

When I asked him why we were not reading the remaining thirty-six books, he said, "Those are for Christians."

His explanations still made no sense to me; I didn't understand why I was not permitted to read the whole book, as I didn't yet grasp the differences between the religions.

He told me those forty-six books were broken into five volumes: Books of Law (the five Books of Moses), Books of History, Books of Psalms (Songs), Books of Wisdom, and Books of Prophecy. And he made me read those forty-six books seven times. At the time, I also didn't know the significance of repeating the same books seven times. The number seven is significant throughout the Torah and is an important number in Judaism. For example, the creation of the world took place over seven days, the first verse of the Torah has seven words, *Shabbat* (the day of rest) falls on the seventh day of the week, each of the Egyptian plagues lasted seven days, and so on.[12] He put extra emphasis on reading these books on Saturday afternoons, Mondays, and Thursdays.

He told me, "They [other Ethiopians from the north who did not have Jewish ancestry] call us 'Falashas,'" but he expressed to me he didn't like being called that because of its derogatory nuance. (The root of Falasha is the Ge'ez word, *Falash*, which means to wander, for example as exiles.)

Gideon believed his religion was the true biblical version. He taught me about priestly sacrifice, Sabbath observance, dietary laws, menstrual separation, fasting, and the significance of Esther. In the Old Testament, the story of Esther is "a potent reminder of the real power of God to deliver people, as well as the ability of just one or two seemingly powerless people to be instruments of deliverance."[13]

Gideon was teaching me Ge'ez and Judaism rather than the Amharic or Hebrew languages, and I was confused. He had told me that to learn Amharic, I had to learn Ge'ez first. I felt like someone who had been sent to study Italian but was faced with learning the Latin language simply because the Italian language is derived from Latin. Latin is the language of religion, though, and knowing Latin is not necessary for learning the Italian spoken on the streets. I felt the same about Ge'ez—that it was a language only for religion and it was not necessary for me to learn it. I just wanted to learn Amharic.

He seemed upset about what Anglican and Protestant Christians had done to his ancestors' religion and the Jewish community in Ethiopia. Now, as I reflect on his manner and methods of teaching, I would say that they were his way of bringing back his religion and imposing it on me. He seemed to want to claim me as part of his ethnic group and place onto me the responsibility of helping to keep his religion alive. He didn't teach me Christianity. In fact, he insisted that I stop reading beyond the defined books and only focus on Judaism.

Basherahil

Like many Arabs, Yemeni-Hadhrami families are keen on making sure their children learn Arabic. Between the ages of five and a half and eight, I was also in intense private schooling to study Arabic.

There were no Arabic schools during those days. Most of the teachings were done at the mosques. My Arabic teacher was a Hadhrami immigrant who worked with other Hadhrami merchants in the leather business. His name was Basherahil; he was related to the Basherahil family my mother worked for as a nanny prior to my birth. Most Hadhramis refer to each other by family names while Ethiopians refer to people by their first names, so I was asked to refer to him as Ustaz (Teacher) Basherahil. Later, I found out his first name was Omer.

Unlike Gideon, my Arabic teacher didn't ask me any questions about my parents. He already knew my biological mother and my father, too. He had much lighter skin than Gideon and often wore a turban. I was always amazed at how he crossed his legs and sat on the floor, which I was also expected to do. Arab men often squat or sit on the floor with stretched or folded legs, cross-legged, or with their legs to the side.

And he was always clean. Personal hygiene is extremely important to Arabs for both spiritual and practical reasons. Because meals are frequently eaten by hand, it is typical to wash the hands before and after eating. And *Wudu*, a minor ablution—the formal washing of the face, hands, and forearms—is required before daily prayers.

In the same way I was taught Amharic, the Arabic language lessons started with the alphabet. Then I moved on to words using pictures and simple sentences.

My Arabic teacher didn't lead me to read the Qur'an, but he was strict about the protocols: being in the state of cleanliness, beginning the recitation with *Ta'awwudh*,[14] slow recitation, accurate pronunciation, beautiful and rhythmic recitation, isolating yourself during recitation, pondering on verses, memorization, and the practices of handling and daily recitation of the Qur'an.

There are several rules for handling the Qur'an:

- *One must have clean hands to touch the Qur'an.*

- *One must keep the Qur'an out of latrines.*

- *One must keep the Qur'an off the floor.*

- *One must use a cloth or plastic dustcover for the Qur'an when it's not in use.*

- *One must keep Qur'an texts on the highest book shelf.*

- *One must place nothing on top of the Qur'an.*

- *One must recite "I seek refuge in God from Satan, the rejected enemy" prior to reading the Qur'an.*

- *One must remain seated on the floor when reading the Qur'an.*

- *One must place the text on a book rest or holder or, if no holder is available, hold the Qur'an above the lap or above waist level.*

- *Women who are menstruating must not hold the Qur'an.*

The first and foremost obligatory practice that my teacher ordered me to carry out was cleansing myself before touching or reciting the Holy Qur'an. The hygiene requirements for the recitation of Holy Qur'an consist of a major ablution called *Ghusl* and the minor ablution, *Wudu*. He mentioned that ablutions must be carried out by doing Ghusl followed by Wudu.

He taught me the Five Pillars of Islam: profession of the *shahada* (faith), *salat* (prayer), *Eid* (alms), *sawm* (fasting), and *Hajj* (pilgrimage). Part of his teaching also included the Islamic way of praying. There are five of prayers each day: *Fajr* (dawn), *Dhuhr* (midday), *Asr* (afternoon), *Maghrib* (sunset), and *Isha* (night). There are also additional required prayers: the Eid prayers, as well as *Taraweeh*[15] and *salat al Janazah*.[16]

The Qur'an had been revealed by God through the angel Gabriel to the Prophet Muhammed (pbuh) in Arabic, which was a complicated language for me at that age. The slightest change in pronunciation of an Arabic word gives rise to a completely different and out-of-context meaning. Therefore, it is necessary that the reader be cautious while pronouncing words of verses from the Qur'an; the reader must ensure that the words are correctly pronounced so as to not misrepresent meanings and messages.

When I mentioned my confusion about the Arabic language and asked my teacher for clarification, he gave me the following explanation:

The Semitic languages were named after Shem, one of Noah's sons, and they are divided into three parts:

1. *An eastern Semitic language is represented by the Akkadian language spread throughout Mesopotamia (the Tigris and Euphrates), and the oldest text was the famous Hammurabi Code.17*

2. *A northwestern Semitic language is represented by the Aramaic language, and its Nabataean Mandaean dialect is Syriac. It is also represented by the Canaanite language, which branched into the Phoenician Ugaritic Hebrew.*

3. *A southwestern Semitic language is represented by the Abyssinian language and its Amharic dialects, and by the Arabic language.*

The Arabic language is divided into two languages:

1. *A southern Arabic language called the Himyarite language. Its dialects are Sabaic and Ma'in, languages that have ceased to exist.*

2. *A northern Arabic language called the classical western language, in which the Noble Qur'an was revealed.*

And the Arabic language, according to my teacher, is the root of all these Semitic languages.

My Arabic and Amharic teachers were at conflict with each other, like divorced parents fighting over a child, each claiming that their religion was the true religion. I wasn't sure who to believe. Ditto for my identity—both wanted to claim me as belonging to their ethnic group. Gideon thought I was a Jew, and Basherahil insisted I was an Arab, so I should be Muslim. Both were trying to convince me that I was one but not the other. Because of their devotion to their respective religions, the teachings were intense on me from both sides. Being the unwilling and unwitting rope in their tug-of-war only served to add to my confusion.

*

I don't profess to know more than what I remember being taught as a child. I'm not a religious scholar or an expert in theology. From my experience, I can only say that Christianity emerged out of Judaism, and Islam is deeply indebted to both Judaism and Christianity. They all are family, and I am still unable to reconcile why humans focus on the differences rather than the similarities.

VII

Orphaned and Homeless

For a child, the loss of a parent is the loss of memory itself.

— Svetlana Alexievich

*A*s I got older, around the age of seven, I found it interesting that I felt I had an upper hand in both schools that I attended. In my elementary school, the Oromo kids didn't understand Amharic, and vice versa, so the Oromo and Amharic boys couldn't communicate with each other. However, I was an anomaly; I could speak with children from both cultures. I could insult any of my classmates in a language they didn't understand, which gave me power, and as a boy of small stature and mixed race, I needed an advantage.

In Ethiopian culture, to say you are the son of a woman is an insult. Unless you are raised by a man, you are not a man. If you're raised by a woman, you are incomplete. Ironically, other than the short periods of time I spent with my father and then my uncle, I was raised by several women, a fact that I'm proud of. They raised me well, and they were strong, positive influences on me.

I used to trigger fights between boys, pitting them against each other with the information I was telling them. Most of the comments I would make were silly, but one of the most significant tools I used was a common Ethiopian insult and one of the most offensive comments an Ethiopian could say to another—to insult someone's mother. I would tell various boys that another party insulted his mother, which would prompt a fight. Fights were normal and regular events amongst boys, as is typical in any culture.

I also found spending time in one house and having a certain kind of meal and then going to the other type of house and eating another ethnic meal was very cool. Because of the requirement for Muslims to eat halal meat, most Christians didn't eat meat at an Islamic family's house, and vice versa. If a cow was slaughtered by a Muslim family, no Christian family would touch it. But I was able to eat anything because I wasn't strictly following any religion.

Ditto for other religious protocols. I moved between the two religions and cultures without boundaries. Both my Amharic and Arabic teachers had taught me that their religion was the correct one—that if I followed the other religion instead of theirs, I would suffer the consequences accordingly. But I quickly learned that if I followed the rules of one religion instead of the other, nothing bad happened to me! I felt as though I were a magician, and this idea was adopted by the other kids, as well. My classmates were waiting with fascination to see what happened to me. The Muslim children expected me to get sick from eating non-halal meat, for example, but I shocked them all by showing up alive the next day! I was living in both worlds, and this also gave me a sense of power and freedom that other children didn't possess.

Abandoned Again

My uncle and I didn't seem to get along very well. He used to give me peculiar looks, and he often shouted derogatory comments at me about my race. As was the case with many Ethiopians his generation, he didn't have a high opinion of Arabs, so he constantly reminded me that I was "a camel-pushing, Arab desert man who has no value and has no place in our society."

I had always been told my father was British, so I told my uncle, "I'm not an Arab."

He would bark back at me, "What do you think of yourself? You *are* an Arab. Your father happened to be living in a British colony and that's why he obtained a British passport. He's an Arab through and through."

He continued to verbally assault me day in and day out, and my dislike of my uncle continued to grow. I began to wish he wouldn't come home; I wanted him to die in an accident somewhere. I asked myself why I was living with him and why he was treating me in such a way—what did I do to him? And I also wondered where my mother was.

From the time I was left with my uncle, all the maids and everyone knew why I was there, but I didn't understand why I had been sent to live with this awful man. The morning after my first night at his house, my bed was wet. His constant verbal abuse from that first night only compounded my confusion and distress.

By the time I was eight, my uncle had divorced his wife. He also dismissed the maids, the guard, and the gardener. He had a mistress, and she moved in with him, but she didn't stay long—maybe a few months. With him in the house alone except for me, I was now expected to cover the house chores, for example, getting milk and assisting with watering the fruit plants. At the same time, the Basherahil families (the Arab family my mother had worked for, and my Arabic teacher, who was also part of the extended Basherahil family) moved to the city of Dire Dawah, about 376 kilometers (234 miles) from where I was. With their move, the option for me to leave and live with other family members in South Yemen became remote, and I was confined to my uncle's house.

My uncle ended up having financial problems with the local banks and other financial institutions, and they began looking for him. Somehow, he had ended up losing all of the money he had stolen from my father's estate. One night I saw him sitting on a chair by the gate in front of the house, holding a rifle. That was the last time I saw him until years later. He left at dawn the next morning—he suddenly vanished from the house, leaving me with no money, food, or any assistance. I was eight years old and had zero support.

I was going to school on an empty stomach. I quickly realized the only way I could possibly survive was by selling some of the household furniture, tools, etc. at the local market to make money.

I'm alone! I have no one! I must survive! were my main thoughts at that time.

After taking over my father's assets, my uncle had purchased a large volume of tools. Construction workers didn't come to work on projects with tools at that time. Rather, they borrowed or leased the tools to perform most construction work. I would say there were no fewer than twenty hammers, tape measures, saws, axes, etc. left behind in his house.

I started by just taking a hammer or measurement tools—any kind of small carpenter items—to a local market and selling them for whatever amount people would pay. The people who intended to buy those items from me were assuming I stole them. Some of the adults physically threatened and frightened me and took the items without paying for them. Other times, they asked why I was selling stuff, and when I told them the truth, they gave me only a small portion of the value of the item. In other cases, I exchanged the items for a loaf of bread. Six months passed by the time I had completely liquidated the house of tools and furnishings, and there was nothing left to be sold.

Having emptied the house, I had run out of options and had no other place to go. I was living alone in an abandoned house and attended school for half the day. During the rest of the day, I roamed around the local market to find some leftover fruit, corn, potatoes, or something I could steal—just quickly grab it and run. At the same time, I had entire freedom, and most children in the neighborhood enjoyed coming to my house so they could play. My uncle's house also had a backyard with about 1,500 square meters (1640 square feet) where he had grown grapes, papaya, and other tropical fruits and plants, including qat, a type of tobacco that most Somali and Arab people—men and women—chew.

I realized I could sell the fruit or exchange it for other food items—whatever it took to support myself. I befriended a lot of adults who could do business with me. My fruit-peddling business lasted for three to six months because most of these fruits are only in season for a short time.

One day a man came to the house to buy fruit. I remember he brought a basket to take the fruit so he could resell it. He looked strange. After he took all the grapes I had, filling his basket, he asked me where the adults lived. I told him they were presently out for business and informed him that I could sell the fruit and collect the money while they were out.

He kind of suspected I wasn't telling the truth. The man approached me, picked me up, and put me against the wall. He started to tell me horrible things to intimidate me.

"LET ME GO! LET ME GO," I shouted, and he put me down.

He took the basket full of grapes and walked away without paying me. As a result, I had nothing to eat, and nothing left to sell from around the house or garden.

Shortly after that, the bank confiscated the house and sealed the doors. I was homeless and truly alone.

*

I had begun to wet the bed when I went to live with my uncle after my father died, but then it stopped when I was alone and living on street.

My uncle was the most abusive human I have known in my life. He had a deep hatred toward Arabs. From the moment he took on the responsibility of raising me, he was unkind to me. He verbally abused me day in and day out even though he had no reason to do so. I wasn't a bad boy or mischievous. I hadn't done anything wrong when I moved in with him at the age of five and a half. In fact, I was unsure, timid, and scared when I was taken to his place. The move to his house was my first encounter with separation, and I always wondered why he continued to be so angry at me without any reason. As I got older, I started to rationalize his treatment of me by saying, "My father was a foreign, Arab, non-Christian man." I thought his hatred was based on my ethnicity and race. I also started to wonder if he was angry at my father for impregnating his younger sister and was taking his shame and anger out on me. I still don't know the answer.

My uncle had agreed to take care of me not out of concern for me but to obtain power of attorney from my mother and take control of my father's estate. He was out for financial gain, and I was simply a tool that he used to embezzle money from the estate. Once he had blown through my father's money, I was no longer of any use to him. With lenders coming after him for repayment of loans he had taken out, he was ashamed and disgraced. He left without notifying anyone that he was leaving. He just left, so no one knew I had been left to fend for myself in his house.

Similar to the Tahir and Mola families, my uncle's fate wasn't any better. He was married numerous times and had many children. None of his children lived past the age of twenty; nor did he ever hold a steady job. Rather, he died broke in the early 1980s.

During my trip in 2010, when I asked my mother about him, she said, "He passed away several years ago." My unfiltered response to her was, "That is good!" Of course, my mother had no knowledge of what happened to me in Nazreth, and she was a bit perplexed about my out-of-character response. All parties who took advantage of my father's death for whatever money there was didn't live long after they had done so, and it satisfied me that they weren't around long enough to enjoy the life they stole from me and my half siblings.

*

I reached out to Ms. Abebech, the lady next door, who was selling home-based alcohol called *areki,* one of the most common alcoholic drinks in Ethiopia, and one of the strongest at 70 percent. One of the distinctions of areki is that most of it is made by women in their homes.

Like gin or vodka, areki is a clear, colorless alcohol made from fermented plants. The leaves of *gesho,* a plant similar to hops, found from Eritrea to South Africa, are ground into a powder and mixed with powdered *bikil* (malt) and water. The fluid is then set aside to ferment for about five days. Then, water is added to powdered *dagussa* (millet) and kneaded to make a dough, which is then baked into cakes. While they are still hot, the cakes are broken into pieces and combined with the fluid. More water is added, and once mixed, the concoction is set aside to ferment for about more four days. After it has fermented, it is distilled and is then known as *terra-areki. Dagim,* in Amharic, means "second time." Another type of areki, *dagim-areki*, is prepared in the same way as terra-areki but is distilled a second time and is stronger than terra-areki.

I offered to assist Ms. Abebech with house chores if she let me stay at her house. She asked me about the house I was staying in as it seemed to be quieter lately and she hadn't seen my father.

I corrected her, "He's not my father. He is my uncle, and he's out of town." I also told her the house was sealed.

"When will he be back?" she asked me.

"I don't know."

After a long pause, finally she said, "Yes, you can stay in my house as long as you don't steal anything."

I assured her, "I won't steal anything. I won't do anything. I'm just cold, and I don't want to be scared and alone."

"How old are you?" she asked.

"I'm almost nine."

"You shouldn't be left home alone. When is your uncle coming back?" she asked again.

"I don't know. Maybe in two or three months," I replied.

"What kind of human is he to leave a young child like you home alone without telling anybody? Where is your mother?"

"She's in Addis Ababa."

She was kind of surprised at my situation, and she agreed to let me into her house.

Ms. Abebech was a tall woman with huge buck teeth, and she was kind. She had a daughter who was around fourteen and a son who was five years old. I heard her saying that between those two surviving children she had lost many children at infancy.

The boy liked to play with me, and he thought I was a magical person because I was nine and he was only five; he looked up to me. In addition, I was the only person he ever saw who was able to read and write, do math, or beat adults in the games that I played.

Ms. Abebech continuously asked me when my uncle was coming home. I always told her I didn't know, and she would say, "You know what? I'm glad you are here. Don't be afraid."

From that point on, I started feeling that I had this lady as a family to assist me, and I was okay. At least I was not alone in a four-bedroom house.

I stayed with her for around sixteen months in the tiny shack she lived in, which consisted of one room separated by a curtain. There was no running water in her house. By this time, all the clothing I had was worn out. Ditto for the shoes. I started walking barefoot because I had outgrown my shoes and had no money to buy new ones. I was floundering around barefoot and unbathed—I perhaps washed myself in the river once during the period of one year.

Ms. Abebech was helping with shelter and often provided me one meal a day. However, she was unable to pay school fees or purchase school supplies for me. As a result, I dropped out of school for two semesters. I spent my time on the street scavenging for food. I was nine years old, and it was a period when surviving day by day was a key task and my priority; attending school wasn't.

*

Abandonment is a wound that never heals. I say only that an abandoned child never forgets. The most important lessons abandonment taught me was that I had basically ditched any hopes of having any adult role models in my life at the time, and I had no trust for adults. I don't think I was born a rebel; I suspect having been abandoned was the major contributing factor for my rebellion and the strong mental attitudes I still possess today.

VIII

Hope

The very least you can do in your life is figure out what you hope for. And the most you can do is live inside that hope. Not admire it from a distance but live right in it, under its roof.

— Barbara Kingsolver

When other children asked me about my parents, I used to tell them both were dead. That was my way of dealing with questions I was unable to answer or didn't want to answer. It was easy to say my father was dead, as he was dead and buried. I was able to make up stories based on what I could recall about his death and the conversations I had overheard about his death. The hardest part was to come up with a story about how my mother died. To admit I had been abandoned would have been the worst thing for my friends to know. I couldn't keep track of the number of lies I was telling the other children about my mother's death, so I often shared conflicting stories. A couple of children who heard me responding to the same question from others about my mother's death had to correct me because the story I had told them was different.

Over time, after repeatedly going through the same feelings and thoughts and telling the stories about my parents, I ended up almost accepting the death of my mother to be true in my own mind. I stopped feeling unwanted. I stopped feeling sad about not having any family members near me. I was certainly happy to be free from the constant abuse my uncle had flung at me. Although I was confused about every question I had in my mind, I also realized I was alone, which was frightening but also empowering. I decided I wouldn't ask for assistance other than sleeping at Ms. Abebech's house because asking for help was a sign of vulnerability and required me to share more of myself than I wanted to. I didn't want anyone to know that I was alone and weak. I suspected that if others knew that I didn't have support from family, they may attack or kill me. Keeping information about my parents to myself was how I kept my status amongst the other children.

I have nothing. I'm alone. I am the only one for me!

Gebeta

One day when I was living at Ms. Abebech's house, I was playing *gebeta* with a group of seven or eight children near my uncle's house. While we were playing, a guy approximately thirty-five to forty years old approached the house looking for the inhabitants. I noticed he was escorted by two others. First, I thought they were bank people, but the two escorts were police officers.

I asked this man why he was there and who he was looking for.

He said, "I'm looking for the owner of the house," and he mentioned my uncle's name.

"That is my uncle, and my name is Adel. What are you looking for?"

"I'm looking for him because I have a problem with the police. I had a car accident, and they confiscated my car, so I need someone to bail me out," the man explained.

I didn't want to tell this man that my uncle had been gone for almost two years because I didn't know him, and I was becoming more concerned about what would happen if I told him the truth. But I also thought he could have been related to my uncle, and if I lied, he would get me in trouble with my uncle, whom I still thought might return one day.

So, I told him, "My uncle is out of town. I don't know when he'll be back."

He asked me, "Did you say he is your uncle?"

"Yes," I said.

"Who's your mother?" he then asked.

"My mother is Weinishet."

"Are you Weinny's son?"

I said I was, and then he asked, "Are you Majid's son?"

"Yes."

"Okay. I knew your father, Majid. He was a gentleman," he told me.

Then he looked at me again with a sad look. He seemed to be more concerned about me at that point than the car accident. He gave me one dollar.

"Thank you," I said to him and gave him an ear-to-ear smile!

He and the two police officers laughed and left the vicinity. I continued to play with the children and as usual, I won the game.

*

Gebeta refers to a group of ancient African board games called *mancala*, which are played with small stones, beans, or seeds, and rows of small holes in the earth, a board, or some other playing surface. The games are played with two players, and the objective is to capture more stones than your opponent. It's a simple mathematical problem, and once you master the strategy of the game, you never lose; you can easily clean everyone out.

Mancala is one of the oldest games, and variations of it are still widely played today around the world. Archaeological evidence suggests the game was played in ancient Egypt. There is also evidence of the game being played in Israel "in the city of Gedera in an excavated Roman bathhouse, where pottery boards and rock cuts were unearthed dating back to between the second and third century AD."[1] Pottery fragments of a board and several rocks (playing pieces) were also found Matara (Eritrea) and Yeha (Ethiopia) dating back to the sixth and seventh centuries AD.[2]

Migration and trade over the past several hundred years brought mancala to other countries and continents, including the Baltic area. It was once popular in Bosnia, where it is called Ban-Ban, as well as Serbia and Greece.

"Two mancala tables from the early eighteenth century are to be found [sic] in Weikersheim Castle in southern Germany. In Western Europe, it never caught on, but was documented by Oxford University orientalist Thomas Hyde."[3]

The game also made its way across the Atlantic.

> *A traditional mancala game called warra was still played in Louisiana in the early 20th century, and a commercial version called kalah became popular in the 1940s. In Cape Verde, mancala is known as ouril. It is played in the Islands [Cape Verde, an island country in the Atlantic ocean] and was brought to the United States by Cape Verdean immigrants. It is played to this day in Cape Verdean communities in New England.4*

Often, I would bet with my opponents, and the loser gave me either fruit or a piece of bread. I was good at this game, and everyone lined up to beat me. However, since I was always winning, my opponents rotated, and I always continued to play until I lost. In addition to the benefit of winning food, this game also helped me learn mathematics.

Claimed

There were not many taxis in those days, and hardly any cars were used to transport people from point A to point B in Nazreth. A horse carriage was the typical transportation.

One afternoon, a horse carriage came by, and as I watched, it pulled over and parked in front of my uncle's house. For about twenty seconds, I tried to figure out who the person inside the carriage was.

My first thought was that my uncle had come back, but a lady exited and walked toward me. I had no recollection of meeting her in the past. I gathered my courage and asked her what or who she was looking for. She didn't answer.

She didn't recognize me, and I didn't recognize her.

The lady paid the horse carriage driver, and after thanking him, she asked him to leave. Then she looked at me and walked away from me toward the gate of the house.

The main gate and the house door were locked because the bank had taken possession of the house, and I didn't have the key.

Again, I asked her, "What are you looking for?"

"This is my brother's house. I came to see him," she said.

"Is my uncle your brother?" I asked her.

"Is the owner of this house your uncle?" she asked.

I replied, "Yes. This is my uncle's house. I am the son of his sister."

She paused, looking at me, and then said, "Then that makes me your auntie."

"Did you say that you are my mother's sister?" I asked.

"Yes. I am the younger sister of your mother," she confirmed, and I saw a sad look on her face. A couple of tears dropped from her eyes.

"Why are you crying?"

"Adel, I am your auntie. I have known you since you were a baby. You have changed. You look different. You look like a homeless person."

And she continued to cry as she hugged me. I was ecstatic and dumbfounded to discover a relative from either of my parents' side because I never knew I had other relatives.

"I've been here alone for almost two years, and I am ten years old." I smiled at her, but I didn't cry. In fact, I barely cried at any point during my childhood. I always tried to remain strong, suppressing my emotions and focusing on survival.

She held my hand, and we walked to the nearest shop, where she bought me a slice of bread and Fanta, a soft drink that most children drank at that time. I was so excited and was anticipating that I would be able to have fun with her.

"What's your name?" I asked her.

"My name is Emebet."

"Thank you for buying me Fanta and the bread," I said to her.

She sat with me on a stone, and she started asking me questions.

"When was the last time you had a meal?" she asked me.

"I eat every other day."

"Where do you sleep?" she continued.

"At my neighbor's house."

She made sure I finished my bread and the Fanta. When I was finished, she returned the empty bottle to the shopkeeper, and then we went to see my neighbor, Ms. Abebech, together. The two women exchanged greetings, and the lady introduced herself by saying who she was—Adel's aunt.

My aunt thanked my neighbor for allowing me to stay in her house. They talked for about fifteen or twenty minutes, and Ms. Abebech told my aunt that my uncle had left me alone, so she took me in and had been letting me stay at her place for more than a year. Almost two years had passed since my uncle had disappeared without word to anyone, and no one in my family knew I had been left to fend for myself.

"He's a fine boy, and he hasn't quit going to school. He hasn't stolen anything from me," she assured my aunt. "He gets along with my children just fine. The neighbors like him too, and the neighborhood children are friends with him. I'm glad you came to see him. I have been wondering when his relatives will come to find him. I don't have the means to buy him shoes or additional clothing. But I'm happy you came to see him. If I may ask, where is his mother?"

My aunt responded, "She is in Addis Ababa. She is married, and she has a couple of children from a different father. Her husband is not a friendly or kind person, and I don't think he wants to have her son live with her now."

By that time, I realized, "Yes, I do have a mother. Where is she anyway?" I asked.

They ignored me.

"How did you find out about him now?" asked Ms. Abebech.

"I heard about Adel's situation from Gashe Negatu, one of our relatives who came here looking for my brother a few weeks ago," she said. "He told us that if something happened to that boy and he died, we can't cry or even say he was part of our family since no one in our family has been looking after him. No one has claimed him, so if something terrible happens to him, my relative said we have no right to mourn him since we didn't look after him when he was alive. That is what prompted me to come to find out the truth about this boy."

She told us she would go back to Addis Ababa and consult with her husband as to whether he would be okay with me going back with her.

"I will probably return to pick him up and take him back to my home to live with us," she said.

Ms. Abebech said, "That would be wonderful. I hope your husband will have a good heart and will let him stay with you. I like him, but I'm not his family, and I can't take proper care of him as I need to support my own children. I'm sure he misses his mother, too. Where is his father anyway?"

The funny thing was that Ms. Abebech had never asked me about my father until this moment. And I never wanted to talk about my family anyway. My aunt told her that my father had died. She explained that my father was from a different country, and that was why I had a peculiar name.

"When I take him to Addis Ababa, I am considering changing his name to an Ethiopian name."

Ms. Abebech replied, "No wonder. I was wondering a little bit about his name, and I also know he kind of speaks another language."

She was referring to Arabic, but she didn't know that's what the language was. She often saw me doing Arabic homework (Qur'an verses), so she was aware that I knew a different language.

Ms. Abebech went on to tell my aunt, "His growth will be stunted due to malnutrition. He was very skinny—just skin and bones—when I let him start spending nights at my house. Often, I give him supper, but I can't afford to feed him all the time. Why is he so skinny?"

My aunt explained, "He was born two months premature. They had to wait a couple of years to even circumcise him, as they didn't think he would survive the cut. I heard he was a very tiny but wiry child. He is small for his age but was expected to be tall like his father."

My aunt had coffee with Ms. Abebech, and then she asked me to go get her a rental horse carriage to take her back to the bus station. I was so happy to see her, and I was impressed she bought me bread and a soft drink, so I rushed out like a rabbit and got her a horse carriage to take her to the station.

*

When reflecting on my life between the ages of eight and ten, I can assure you, I was more optimistic than hopeful. Deep down, I felt something good would happen or just like a bad storm, my situation would dissipate. Back then, yes, my way of thinking wasn't developed; my natural instincts weren't any better than those of an animal. Animals are more flexible in their outlook. Therefore, just like an animal, I easily adapted to my changing circumstances. I alternated between my optimistic and pessimistic perspective to allow me to best adapt to my changing environment.

Hope

IX

Rescued

Our most basic instinct is not for survival but for family. Most of us would give our own life for the survival of a family member, yet we lead our daily life too often as if we take our family for granted.

— Paul Pearshall

*I*n September 1972, when I was ten years old, my aunt Emebet returned to Nazreth from Addis Ababa. This time there were no surprises, and no introductions were required. I instantly recognized her as my aunt, the younger sister of my mother.

I remembered that the last time she visited us, she mentioned she would ask her husband if it would be okay with him for me to move in with them in Addis Ababa. When she returned, I wasn't sure if she was planning to take me to Addis Ababa or if she had come to say that she was sorry, "I won't be able to take you." As soon as she entered Ms. Abebech's house, I was eager to know the verdict. She told us her husband agreed I was to stay with his family.

After having exchanged greetings with Ms. Abebech, Emebet said she would rather return to Addis Ababa before the day was out because she had an infant at home. Ms. Abebech insisted that she at least spend the night and we both go early in the morning after having rested and eaten a meal. I was so anxious to get up and leave, and I had nothing to pack or deal with. I was ready to go and start this new chapter of my life with decent family members! Emebet insisted on returning home right away, as she had her own young children she needed to attend to, and so we left.

*

That was the last time I saw Ms. Abebech. When I returned to Ethiopia with my daughters in 2010, I went to her home to seek her out. Sadly, in the thirty-eight years since I left her home, both she and her oldest daughter had passed away. My daughters and I waited for an hour and a half to see if her son would come home, but he didn't. I'm saddened that I didn't get the chance, as an adult, to thank Ms. Abebech for her generosity and support when I so desperately needed it.

*

Had my aunt not told Ms. Abebech that she had an infant child at home, it's possible that Ms. Abebech, being the generous, kind woman that she was, may have said to my aunt, "Afer sihon; please stay overnight at my house." *Afer* means a ground or soil, and *sihon* means beneath, and so the literal translation of the phrase afer sihon is "bowing beneath the ground or under the soil." Without cultural context, that phrase seems ambiguous and odd and is perhaps meaningless. However, afer sihon does have a deep meaning.

> *Walking in sandals on the filthy roads of Israel in the*
> *first century made it imperative that feet be washed*
> *before a communal meal, especially since people reclined*
> *at a low table and feet were very much in evidence. When*
> *Jesus rose from the table and began to wash the feet of*
> *the disciples (John 13:4), He was doing the work of the*
> *lowliest of servants. The disciples must have been*
> *stunned at this act of humility and condescension, that*
> *Christ, their Lord and master, should wash the feet of*
> *His disciples, when it was their proper work to have*
> *washed His. … The humility expressed by His act with*
> *towel and basin foreshadowed His ultimate act of*
> *humility and love on the cross.[1]*

To wash someone's feet or shine their shoes shows humility and servitude. Likewise, to say aferi sihoni to someone means you are telling them you are humbling yourself to them. When inviting someone to a meal or to stay at your home overnight, including aferi sihoni in your invitation would be similar to saying, "I not worthy of eating with you or having you as a guest in my home, but I would be honored if you would join me." But it means so much more than this.

In Ethiopia, when someone invites you to a meal, the expected response is, "Thank you but I have already eaten," even if you haven't eaten for days! However, when someone says aferi sihoni to you, you cannot refuse their invitation because they have lowered themselves so deeply that they are metaphorically "under the soil." If you can imagine lying down on the ground to minimize yourself—your importance—consider that going below the soil shows an even greater depth of humility. You are not only lowering yourself; you are showing that you are not above getting dirty for the other person, as Jesus did with his disciples.

*

My aunt and I walked to the train station to catch the train that connected the city of Nazreth to Addis Ababa. She purchased a passenger ticket for herself, and since I was under the age of twelve, I was able to ride for free. The train ride to Addis Ababa seemed to take about an hour. I sat by the window watching everything that passed by. As the scenery came and went outside the window, I thought it looked like the trees were running away from the train rather than the train moving through the valleys. Even though I had been on the train in the past, that is the only recollection I have about any train rides up to that point.

Her house was approximately three kilometers (1.9 miles) from the main train station in Addis Ababa. I had been five and a half years old when I left Addis Ababa, and now that another five years had passed, I didn't recognize any of the buildings. Maybe the city hadn't changed much, or even at all, but I was too young to recall what the city had looked like back when I first lived there.

As we walked past office buildings, hotels, airline agents, and shops, I couldn't help but be captivated. In comparison to Addis Ababa, Nazreth was more of a small village with farms and cattle. We would be lucky to see one car driving by in our neighborhood. We had to walk a few miles in order to see cars on the main roads. With the exception of a few houses like the one my uncle and I lived in, most homes were mud huts. Arriving in the capital and seeing modern office buildings, apartments, paved roads, cars, and people wearing suits filled me with the same excitement and wonder that a child might experience going to Disneyland or visiting a science center or zoo for the first time.

By this time, I was able to read a few English words and sentences. I read something saying, "Ethiopian Communication Building" and "Ras Hotel" on our way. I was so mesmerized at the small replicas of airplanes in the airline office's windows.

I stopped often, wanting to ask questions. I was so excited, I want to see, touch, and learn about everything around me, but my aunt was annoyed with my dawdling and gawking, and she pushed me along.

"Hurry up. We're late. We've got to go."

I kept looking at everything, unperturbed by the fact that I was walking on the street barefoot.

At the time, my aunt was living in a neighborhood called Filwoha, where the Sheraton Hotel complex now stands. When we arrived at her house, I saw three children—a boy, aged four, and two girls, aged three and two. I also noticed a teenaged boy and girl. The girl appeared to be around seventeen, while the boy was about fourteen and not much taller than I was. Both were servants.

My aunt immediately asked me to wash my feet and hands before she introduced me to her children. The male servant kept looking at me. He gave me water to wash my hands and feet, which I did.

When I walked into the house, my aunt said, "Here is my oldest son, Getahun, and his sisters, Meseret and Aynalem."

She went on to introduce me to the two servants and stated that I would be taking over the boy's duties, pointing to the male servant. I had never heard of the word *duties,* and I was wondering what his duties were. I kept glancing at him, and he continued staring at me in silence.

In the early evening hours, her husband arrived home. He had greasy hands. I was wondering what he did to get his hands that dirty. He said hello to me, and he turned his attention to his wife to ask her about her day trip.

After I had lived with my aunt and her husband, Mamecha, for a while, I learned that he was a mechanic who co-owned a car workshop. He and his workers provided mechanical services for FIAT trucks. The workshop had previously been owned by an Italian businessman named Lozzi. When the Italian fellow passed away, three of the senior mechanics, one of whom was my aunt's husband, bought the workshop from the Italian businessman's family. During that time, by Ethiopian standards, to own such a business was a high achievement with an upper middle-class income.

The male servant quickly brought soap and warm water to the man of the house and assisted him with washing his hands. At that moment, I realized this man was my aunt's husband, the father of the children. After washing and drying his hands, he picked up his daughters and kissed them. In the process, I noticed the female servant preparing the dinner table so that the family could gather for supper.[2]

As the family gathered to eat, I was so hungry, and I swiftly pulled a chair to join them. My aunt quickly pointed out to me that I wasn't allowed to sit with them. Rather, I was to wait until after the family had eaten, and I would be having supper with the servants. That didn't make any sense to me, but I obediently retreated from the table.

After the family ate, I sat down with the servants to have my supper. I was disappointed that I had to be seated with the house helpers instead of the family. After all, I thought I was a member of the family. I didn't want to eat at all. Even though there was plenty of food in front of me, I choose to eat little as a form of protest.

A couple of days later, my aunt requested that the male helper teach me his daily chores. The boy got up every morning before anyone else and set off to a small shop to get fresh bottled milk. After breakfast was served, he went to the nearest local market to purchase items required for the female servant to cook the meals. In the afternoon, he assisted the female servant with cleaning the dishes, and at least once a day, he fetched the charcoal that was used to boil coffee. He helped boil the coffee and ensured neighbors were invited to join the coffee sessions.

A week after my training had started, my aunt handed any outstanding cash balance she owed to the male servant and wished him the best. He packed his stuff left.

Although my language skills weren't yet fully developed, I started to write a journal at this time. I didn't call it a journal, nor did I know what journal was, but I decided to write down everything I saw and experienced, including my reflections of what had happened to me in Nazreth.

The purpose in writing my journal was as a means or a venue to speak to someone. I was imagining I was conversing with my dead father or the mother whose location I didn't know. I kept writing records of events without including any emotions or feelings, and I made sure what I wrote was not seen by anyone. I knew my aunt and uncle wouldn't be able to read what I wrote, but I made sure no one saw the journals just in case. When I wrote about specific events or situations, I gave fake names to the characters, and often I mixed Arabic words in between Amharic so that no one would know the subject of my writings.

My writing of journals continues to this day. In January 2020, when I decided to write my memoir, I reached out to members of both sides of my family in South Yemen and Ethiopia to locate and send to me all my journals, letters, and pictures. In all honesty, I didn't think I would recover a single record. Lo and behold, all my forty-seven-year-old handwritten records—dating back to 1973—were located and I received them in two batches: in early 2020 and in June 2021. For my aunt Emebet to keep those records for those many years was a testimony of her love and respect for me. When I asked her what compelled her to keep my letters and notes, she said, "I knew you didn't write useless stuff. I knew you were special and intelligent, and I thought perhaps one of my children would learn something from you." She never learned to read or write, but she has huge respect for education. I told her, "You instilled in me steel determination to finish what I start. I'm a product of your efforts!"

Lucy Dacus said, "A journal is your completely unaltered voice." My childhood journals say so much about me and what was going on inside me in those days. In the absence of a psychologist, my journals were a safe place where I could process and deal with what life was throwing at me. Writing in my journals allowed me to express and emphasize what I was grateful for.

Knowledge is Power

In the meantime, my aunt was looking for an elementary school to enroll me in. The nearest school to her house was a private school named Eyou Beliyou. The school could only accept me for one semester, as one of the students was absent due to medical reasons and they had no room for additional students. When the other student returned to school, I would be dismissed. She agreed to this arrangement.

During this time, I acquainted myself with the neighborhood. I noticed many of the men were glued to radios to listen to coverage of the 1972 Summer Olympics in West Germany. From the family and the neighbors, I learned that an Ethiopian marathon runner was expected to bring home the gold medal for the fourth time in a row.

I started to read the local papers and spent a considerable amount of time reading the sports section. I learned about a barefoot runner named Abebe Bikila, who had become the first Black African to win an Olympic marathon gold medal on the streets of Rome. It was without doubt one of the most iconic moments of the 1960 Games. Setting a new world record … and barefoot!

The papers were quoting Bikila's own words as he crossed the finish line: "I wanted the world to know that my country, Ethiopia, has always won with determination and heroism."

One Italian newspaper wrote, "Italy sent an army to conquer Ethiopia, but Ethiopia sent one Imperial bodyguard to conquer Rome."[3]

When I was older, in my further readings and in watching documentary shows, I read and heard Bob Richards describe it like this:

> *I was working for CBS then, and here in the marathon is this barefoot guy. I mean … how in the world you can run a marathon on cobblestones barefoot? And all the splendor of Rome, here's the Baths of Caracalla, here's the Appian Way, here is the Arc of Constantine. It's so dramatic because the Italian army had taken the symbol of Ethiopia, and it was there and in the light you could see it … I started crying … to me it was one of the most dramatic moments I have ever seen in the Olympics.[4]*

John Kelley finished third in the Rome Olympic marathon and expressed his awe and admiration for Bikila's ability to win the race barefoot on the cobblestones:

> *I had run over those final fifteen kilometers in shoes, and uh, it was not easy. There were cobblestones, some of them quite big. I couldn't imagine taking that shock of barefooted running for fifteen kilometers at the pace that Abebe was running, especially. It must have been an extremely difficult victory.[5]*

Due to a lack of resources, I had to run around barefoot in Nazreth for about thirteen months. I was ashamed about being barefoot everywhere I went until I read the newspaper article about Abebe Bikila. *If he could win an Olympic marathon while running barefoot,* I thought, *maybe I need not be ashamed. After all, there is something good about going barefoot.*

Still, I was pleased when my aunt bought me a pair of shoes about two weeks after I went to live with her, as Addis Ababa was a much colder city with lots of rain. It would have been impossible for me to walk around barefoot indefinitely as I had done in Nazreth. However, my aunt was also strict with the use of the shoes she bought me. They were to only be worn during school trips and to the market, not around the house. And she firmly instructed me that I was definitely not to wear the shoes while playing soccer.

The paper continued to report on Bikila's achievements. In addition to setting the world record while running barefoot, Bikila was also the first athlete to win the Olympic marathon back-to-back, representing Ethiopia in the 1960 and 1964 Olympics. The latter was in Tokyo, though he was wearing shoes in that race. He ran in the Tokyo Olympics under extremely hot and humid conditions. Several athletes collapsed during that marathon, but Bikila not only finished the race, he set a new Olympic record. At the conclusion of the race, he didn't show any signs of fatigue—he did his routine exercise just after crossing the finish line.

His strength and endurance were such that Basil Heatley of Great Britain, who finished second in Tokyo, didn't realize that Abebe Bikila had finished ahead of him until he got to the finish line and saw there was no tape:

> *I didn't see Bikila at all. I entered the stadium knowing only that Tsuburaya was just in front. That was the job to attend to, but I got the advantage because I was coming from behind. I was able to take him by surprise … Bikila, that day, quite honestly was in a class of his own in those conditions. He won the A race and I won the B race.*[6]

Bikila got injured during the 1968 Mexico Olympic marathon, but his countryman won the race giving the country its third consecutive gold medal. Bikila was critically injured in a car accident in 1969, leaving him paralyzed and ultimately contributing to his death in 1973, but he remains a national hero. In 1972, when I was ten, the entire nation was eagerly anticipating that summer's Olympic marathon result. I became excited about and fascinated by his accomplishments, and my interest in running was piqued.

*

Where my aunt lived, about ten rental properties were in a tin-fenced complex with only three washrooms. Two of the washrooms were shared amongst all tenants, and the third was the landlord's. The washrooms were like the outhouses we see at campgrounds in Canada and the US, and trucks came every couple of months to remove the human waste.

Since most people, including my aunt and her husband, didn't know how to read, I was the neighborhood expert who was able to read the reports for my relatives and the neighboring households. That gave me huge self-pride. Many gathered in groups to listen to the radio, but radio programs had specific hours, and it was difficult for most to leave their work and respective chores to listen to the radio when the programs were scheduled. Not to mention, owning a small transistor radio was a privilege for many! The newspaper was a convenient source for all to catch up with the news; once everyone discovered I could read, I was nominated as the complex's news reporter. I was to read and re-read the news coverage when it was convenient for them, so I would sit in the middle of the complex. Members from the other families would gather around me at different times of day, and I would read the newspaper to them.

My role was empowering. Having adults sit and listen to me as I read to them gave me a feeling of power and superiority—as a child, I was able to do something that most adults could not do. I knew then that reading was a powerful key to knowledge, information, and opportunity. The daily ritual filled me with a huge sense of achievement. I had moved from reading Jewish and Islamic holy books to reading real events, everyday news. I was passing along information to people about events that impacted their lives. I held the key that opened the door to the world for the other people—the adults—in my community!

My aunt's husband, Mamecha, always warned me not to forget the newspaper anywhere and to return it to him once I was finished with it, as he cut the pages into squares to use as toilet paper. Using newspaper squares as toilet paper was a bit of an advantage when so many other people had nothing to use. Arabs and Muslims—both men and women—used their left hands in lieu of toilet paper to wash themselves after using the toilet. In contrast, Ethiopian Christians did not. At that point, I had never seen women take paper to the washroom. Rather, women took a tin of water, perhaps 250 milliliters (one cup), when they went to the washroom twice a day. And I only saw Arab men and women take water to washrooms, not Ethiopian men. The men used newspaper or other related items as toilet paper.

*

In 2014, I ran my first marathon at the age of fifty-two. When I started to take part in marathons, I kept Bikila[7] in my mind, as his accomplishments gave me a sense of motivation and purpose. People often said, "You did very well in your race," and asked, "What is the trick?" My standard responses were, "I kept imagining my ex-wife chasing me," and "I kept envisioning my daughters waiting for me at the finish line." The truth was that I had Abebe Bikila in my mind the entire course.

X

Father Figure

Fathers are so necessary as examples and guides for our children in wisdom and virtue. Without father figures, young people often feel orphaned; left adrift at a critical moment in their growth and development.

— Pope Francis

*A*fter school, instead of returning home, I started to wander around, exploring different aspects of the area. Within a couple of weeks, I discovered the Ethiopian Foreign Affairs Office, the African Union Office, and Meskel Square, a public square in Addis Ababa where people gather for social meetings or for holding demonstrations (see Appendix Three). As I was passing by the shops and offices, I noticed a laundry facility called Zenith, which was run by Greek- or Italian-looking people.

A month or so into the school year, on my daily route home, I summoned up the courage to enter the laundry facility. A tall, light-skinned man was standing behind the counter. I said hello in Amharic. He said hello back to me, and I quickly realized he had a different accent.

"What do you clean here?" I asked him.

Instead of answering my question, he asked why I was there.

"Just wondering," I replied and asked him. "Are you Greek?" Being a bookworm, I always read any book that came my way. Some were about the Ethiopian war against the Italians, and so at that age, I assumed that every person with light-colored skin was either Italian or Greek because there were many Italians and Greeks in Ethiopia at that time. In this case, Bansser, the shopkeeper, did not wear an Arab outfit, which I was accustomed to seeing; rather he wore a European outfit. Therefore, I thought he had to be Greek.

He gave me one quick glance and told me to leave, as he was busy. At that moment, the phone next to him on top of the counter rang and he picked it up. I didn't move. In a few seconds, he started to speak to the other person in both French and Arabic. My curiosity increased. He directed me with his hands to leave the place. I didn't.

After he hung up the phone, he asked me once again with a stern voice to leave his shop.

I told him, "I speak Arabic."

I said a couple of words, primarily "Hello" and "How are you?" followed by "What is your name?" I went on to say, "My father's name was Majid."

At this revelation, he quickly came out from behind the counter and started to ask me more questions. Since my Arabic was weak, I responded back in Amharic with a couple of Oromo words. He asked for the name of my mother and more.

Finally, he gave me a long look and told me, "I knew your father. He was a friend of mine. My countryman."

I thought he was joking.

He said to me, "Come tomorrow. I will show you your father's picture."

I was bewildered and baffled. I hadn't expected anything like this to happen.

"Listen, I'm busy now. Can you come tomorrow after school?" he repeated.

I agreed and departed.

I didn't tell anyone that I had found someone who had known my father. Although he and I didn't have a direct bloodline relationship, this man was from the same village as my father was. Bloodlines are important to Arabs, but significant relationships can also be formed between Yemeni-Hadhrami individuals over time based on trust. He knew my father's family and another close friend of my father's, too, so he was as close as any blood relation could be. Therefore, in my mind, this man was related to me.

I didn't sleep all night thinking about the man I had met. I wasn't sure if he was telling me the truth or if telling me he knew my father was his way of getting rid of me from his workplace, as he thought I was an obnoxious boy, but I was curious and wanted to know more.

The next day, Ahmed Bansser gave a me picture showing four people. Although I had a faded memory of my father, this was the first time, at the age of ten, I was able to see a concrete image of my father. I asked Bansser who the other children and the man standing by him were.

"Those children are your brother, Hussein, and your sister, Fawzia. The man standing by your father was an Indian accountant, Ali Khalil, who worked for your father as office administrator."

Bansser continued to talk, but I was spaced out in my own world. I wanted to speak to the picture and engage these men and children in a conversation. He knew I wasn't listening to him. He tapped me on my shoulder to bring me out of my dreamland.

"You kind of look like your brother, especially around your mouth, but you're much shorter and slim," he told me.

"Where do they live now?" I asked.

"Last I heard, your bother was in Aden working for a major British shipping company, but I've also heard Hussein has moved to Saudi Arabia. I know your sister Fawzia is living in Hadhramaut with your stepmother, Maryam."

I was fascinated by the idea that I had family members elsewhere and started to dream about meeting them one day.

A Noble Man

Bansser was about six feet (183 centimeters) tall. He was an elegant-looking man with the type of business suits, ties, and the Rolex he was wearing. His shoes were perfectly shined and always looked brand new. He never raised his voice and had an all-round kind demeanor. He listened intently, and I used to suspect he may have had a hearing problem. When he walked around his laundry facility, he put both hands behind him. When customers handed him clothing for dry cleaning, he gave them the utmost respect and customer service: smiles and kind treatment. Even though his customers were rich and influential, every now and then I saw servants and drivers of the wealthier individuals drop off clothing that belonged to those well-to-do-families. Bansser treated those individuals in the same manner as he did their wealthy employers. That was something that I was not accustomed to seeing. Talking or exchanging greetings with the lower class was not something most Ethiopians did during those days.

Zenith, the store, was spotless as workers cleaned the place at night or in the early morning hours before the laundry facility opened. I enjoyed the smell of the cleaning chemicals. It was my first exposure to an orderly store and how the cleaned clothing was kept on the racks. I always wanted to see if the workers were having difficulties finding clothing that had been left at the store for months. The customer brought the receipt, and the clothing was brought to him within minutes. I always asked myself, *How do they know where the clothing items are? How can they find the right items so quickly?*

It's amazing to me still today that I encountered Bansser by chance. At the time, Addis Ababa was a city of two million people. If someone had shown me a picture of him and told me, "Go find this man," I could have scoured the city for days, weeks, or even months looking for him, and chances are I never would have found him. The fact that I randomly stumbled into a shop owned by my father's close friend who had previously helped my mother and other members of my family and would end up becoming my father figure can only mean that I had angels watching over me.

*

During my 2010 trip, I made sure I visited Zenith again. The doors were rusted and the paint on the interior walls was peeling off. The smell of the chemicals was still there, but the ironing boards and the large washing machine clearly exhibited their age. Wear and tear were evident, and I wondered how they managed to keep it functional. The sliding doors where light or bright colored clothing was kept and the counter desk, which I used to stand behind, were worn and looked beaten. A portion of the entrance hallway was partitioned off as an office space for Bansser's only daughter, Fawzia. (She happened to have the same name as one of my older half sisters living in South Yemen.) Regardless of the state of the facility, I was excited to revisit the place and reminisce about my boyhood days. Tears filled my eyes as I recalled where Bansser used to stand and tell me stories about my father. I regretted that he didn't live long enough to see what I had become. Most importantly I mourned for the lost opportunity to ask him more questions about him and my late father, as I am now an adult and a father with a totally different perspective.

Discovery

As I tried to fall asleep that night, I started to think more about my father. I forced myself to remember images of him and reflect on and reminisce about him. My memories were a bit blurry, but some of them were coming back to me. I only remembered a few things—hardly any—but I tried to recall as much as I could.

During the difficult periods in Nazreth and after moving in with my aunt, I had always asked myself, *Where is my mother? What would my life be like if I had parents and was living with them?* Finding this man at the laundry facility was like stumbling upon a new path of discovery. Discovery of my father, whom I had hardly known, and the possibility of knowing who my father was. Discovery of my identity. Wondering if I had siblings from my father's side and if so, how many were there? Where did they live? Did they know I existed, and did they know that I was our father's son? Bansser had said the two children in the picture were my sister and brother; did I really have siblings?

I lay in bed that night thinking and reflecting on what I remembered of how my father walked, talked, looked, and sounded. His brown skin, large body size, and his belly. Most of all, how hairy he was. Yes, he was bald, but he had perfect white teeth. He spoke loudly and was a bit temperamental—somewhat intimidating. I was curious. Confused. Excited. But also scared at what this revelation might mean. It was like suddenly being told I had a million dollars in the bank and having no idea how it came to be or what to do with it. I wondered if what this man had told me was even true; perhaps he told me he knew my father just to get rid of me!

Everyone I knew had parents, at least one. In my case, I had none. I was confused and was struggling within, wondering how I would react to finding my family. My uncle, my mother's older brother, was no use to me, as he was unkind and had left me home alone without telling anyone, but although I was eager to complain about him to anyone from my father's side of the family, I never did. And my aunt viewed and treated me as her servant rather than her nephew.

Would my father's family be as harsh as my mother's side? I had so many thoughts and questions running through my mind all night.

*

The next morning, I was unable to wake early and get the milk from the store because I had been tossing and turning and finally fell asleep in the early hours. When the female servant poured cold water on my head to wake me up, I jumped out of bed and ran to get the milk. Then I went to school totally exhausted. I didn't listen to or comprehend a thing that was discussed in the class that day. All I was thinking about was meeting that interesting man again. I didn't even know his name then, but I knew he held the key to my learning more about my father. School was over by 1:30 p.m., and I scampered off to the laundry again.

The man was there. He smiled when I entered. His teeth had gold fillings, and that was the first time I had seen gold embedded in human teeth. He opened the counter gate and allowed me to proceed to the other side of the counter. He asked me to sit in one of the chairs, and he started to tell me about my father. Most importantly, he was interested to know where I had spent the last five years since my father's death. I provided him with a brief update without getting into many of the details.

The quest to find my relatives in South Yemen and the urge to leave Ethiopia and find a better life were born that day. I saw in front of me the opportunity to connect with relatives I hadn't even known existed. In contrast to having been insulted and told by my mother's brother how useless and unwanted I was, I was excited to learn I had, in fact, come from a decent family. I was at the age when I was seeking acceptance and belonging, and I was on the verge of grabbing onto those things.

The man told me his name was Ahmed Bansser.

*

A few days after we first met, he took me to meet another Hadhrami man named Salem Bagarsh. I also met Bagarsh's son, Abubaker. Salem Bagarsh had migrated from Hadhramaut and once lived in the city of Al-Shihr, where my father was from. Abubaker, his only son, knew my father's other son, my older brother Hussein, as they had attended school together in Addis Ababa.

The most interesting encounter that I will never forget was my first time meeting Bagarsh. He was an African-looking, Black, Yemeni-Hadhrami. He spoke loudly and seemed temperamental. As Bansser and I entered Bagarsh's office, the coffee processing facility, Bagarsh didn't know who I was and why I was there. The two men exchanged small talk. Half an hour into the visit, Bagarsh began smoking a hookah. (*Hookah* is called *shisha* in Yemeni Arabic; it is a water-pipe-stemmed instrument for heating or vaporizing when smoking tobacco.)

Bagarsh gave me a quick look, turned to Bansser, and asked who I was. Bansser chuckled a bit before starting to speak.

And he said, "It's an interesting coincidence that happened a couple of days ago. I ran into him at my dry-cleaning shop. This is Adel. Majid's son."

Bagarsh pulled the hookah pipe out of his mouth and said, "Our Majid? Where did you find him?"

Bansser nodded.

Bagarsh gave me another look and suddenly started screaming at me. "Get out of my office! You're a son of Satan! Get out! You're a son of the beast!"

His voice was deafening, and I turned to run out of his office, having been scolded.

Bansser smiled and told me to wait for him in his car. I was totally confused as to why Bagarsh screamed the way he did. Moreover, I didn't understand why Bansser smiled instead of calming the man down or feeling sorry for me.

While I was sitting in Bansser's car and waiting for his return, I kept wondering whether all Arabs were this way.

What had my father done to this man to make him so upset?

I was also questioning whether Bagarsh was a normal person.

After thirty minutes or so, Bansser sent one of Bagarsh's office clerks to the car and requested that I return to the office. I was scared to go back inside, but I did as I was asked. I went back and sat by Bansser's side.

Bagarsh didn't give me a second look. He kept talking with Bansser.

Once they finished talking, Bansser and I stood up to depart. At that moment, Bagarsh asked me to visit him every now and then. I didn't respond. I feared him, and he also sensed that I was rattled. Finally, Bagarsh said, "Be strong. There is nothing to be scared of."

We left his office.

As we drove back to Bansser's shop, I asked him why Bagarsh was mad at me. He chuckled again and said he would tell me someday.

I felt safe with Bansser. He had taken me under his wing, and it became clear to me that not only was he to be trusted, but he was making the effort to teach me about my father and how to become an Arab man. I was starting to get a better sense of who I was and where I had come from. And I finally had a family. Folks who weren't family members, but my father's countrymen, who I could rely on.

*

When I turned fifteen, Bansser finally told me the true story behind the dispute between my father and Bagarsh. Apparently, my stepmother Maryam, while she was in Ethiopia, wanted to return to South Yemen. My father had refused. She approached Bagarsh to see if he would assist her with travel arrangements. Bagarsh, being kind, managed to help her return to South Yemen with her daughter.

When my father returned home from a business trip, his wife had already left the country. Once he found out when and how she had departed, he was angered and confronted Bagarsh. While this matter cooled off, several months later, a cargo train with a load of coffee derailed enroute to Djibouti. With that, Bagarsh lost all of his assets and investments. He was totally broke. He approached my father to borrow money to re-start his coffee business. My father hadn't forgotten what Bagarsh did to help Maryam leave my father. In return, he told Bagarsh he would lend him money, but with two conditions. The first condition was that Bagarsh shave off my father's pubic hair, and the second was that he allow my father to spend the night with Bagarsh's wife.

Neither condition was met, and ever since then, my father and Bagarsh didn't speak to each other.

Despite such a dispute with my father, Bagarsh let go of all anger toward my father and continued to assist me financially and morally until I departed Ethiopia for South Yemen because he was an honorable man. And because that is what Yemeni-Hadhrami people do to help each other. He knew I needed help, and I was a Yemeni-Hadhrami boy.

*

When I was a boy, one of the first books I read was by Anne Frank. One particular sentence lingered in my mind until this day: "No one has ever become poor by giving." When Bagarsh and Bansser extended their helping hands, they didn't think of being the reason behind my satisfying life; they didn't even live long enough to witness my smiling adult face. I may not remember everything I saw about these men—I have definitely forgotten most of the things they said to me—but I will forever remember their interventions in my times of need.

XI

Regular Kid

Formal education teaches how to stand, but to see the rainbow you must come out and walk many steps on your own.

— Amit Ray

Entrepreneur

After I became more well-known by the other residents in the complex, the neighbors who didn't have children or who couldn't afford to hire servants asked my aunt every now and then if I could do some tasks for them. She agreed. Often, I got rewarded with money and homemade bread.

One day, one of the ladies asked my aunt for permission to take me somewhere. The intent was that I would be sent to this destination in the future to deliver or pick something up for her, but the first time, she would show me where to go and what was to be done there. After that, I would go on my own. I didn't know where we were going, but as long as my aunt agreed to it, I didn't care, nor did I have a choice, anyway.

We must have walked about ten kilometers (six miles) to get to our destination. When we arrived, we entered a house, and the lady from our complex spoke to a man about a couple issues she and some other ladies had, mostly about their husbands' drinking problems. She also mentioned one of her neighbors was unable to get pregnant and was worried that, as a result, her husband would leave her for another woman.

I remembered reading from one of my schoolbooks that people go to a Catholic priest for confession, so this visit made sense to me. The man listened carefully to the issues that were brought to his attention, and as he was listening, he started to write on a piece of paper. I leaned over to see what he was writing. It looked like Arabic, but it was neither Arabic nor Amharic. The scribbles were a kind of mixed-up written words I had never seen before. Reflecting on it now, it reminds me of the shorthand notes most office secretaries used to take during the 1960s and 1970s.

The man's house smelled of incense. He had so many candles, and his clothing was different—neither Arab nor Ethiopian. The smell of the incense gave me a sense of calm and focus. He sat in a similar manner to most Arab men, but not exactly the same, and he wasn't an Arab. His was more of a meditation posture.

After writing these notes with black and red ink by dipping the point of a pen into bottles containing two different inks, he folded the papers in a strange way so that my neighbor couldn't easily unfold and read them. In fact, he created a square-looking shape by coiling the paper.

The lady gave him fifty cents for each paper. He advised her to give these papers to each of the ladies she was talking about and told her how the women should take each of their remedies. There were different instructions for each paper—a different solution for each problem. One woman was to keep her scarf on all the time, another was to put the paper into a glass of water a couple times, and the third one was to wrap the paper around her shoulder. After he repeated the instructions of which lady should take which remedy, my neighbor and I left this man's house.

When I returned home, my aunt asked me how the trip was. I told her it was fine, and I described to her the place and the man.

"He is a warlock. A warlock is a male practitioner of witchcraft," she informed me after hearing my description.

I asked, "What does that mean?"

She said, "A person, and especially a woman, believed to have magic powers."

When I insisted on knowing what she meant, she said, "He is a cunning man—one whom we believe to practice magic for the purposes of good rather than evil." I kept thinking about how this man possessed such magical powers. It wasn't something I was taught about in schools or holy books. My curiosity soared sky high. I anxiously waited for opportunities to visit him again and again.

A couple of trips to this warlock's house inspired me to become an immediate entrepreneur. Before long, when people gave me messages to relay to the man, instead of trekking to his house, I scuttled off and started to write little notes in both Arabic and Amharic and fold them in the same manner as the man was folding his paper. I sold them to the neighbors who told me their problems. Everyone who was sick was healed without knowing I had provided the remedy.

Those who found their problems weren't solved or who were faced with reoccurring matters kept dishing out money to me to pass on to the man … which I didn't do. I kept writing the notes and pocketing the money.

Almost a year later, one of the neighborhood ladies ran into the warlock at the local market and during their conversation, he revealed that I hadn't been to see him for ages. I was belted and tortured with *berbere* smoke. Berbere is a traditional Ethiopian spice blend composed of chiles, garlic, fenugreek, and a handful of warm spices, such as allspice and cinnamon. It is used to cook stew. I was wrapped in a blanket and held upside down by a couple of ladies while my aunt put the berbere powder on hot charcoals. Inhaling the smoke was one of the most bitter experiences I had as a child.

I dissolved my sole proprietorship immediately after receiving that punishment.

*

As a child, I already knew the differences between the Arab and Ethiopian calendar systems.

Ten days after my arrival in Addis Ababa, it was September 11, the Ethiopian New Year. All new Ethiopian music was released on September 11. The popular Ethiopian bands at that time were Police, Imperial Guard, etc. A famous singer named Tilahun Gesses sang the last song of the evening on September 11 that year—1972. He had a beautiful voice.

Mamecha, my aunt's husband, was so impressed, after the song was over, he said, "It would have been better if the Oromo[1] tribe stopped having children after Tilahun." At the time, I didn't comprehend the intended meaning of his comment, and still today after almost fifty years, I ask myself, *Did he say that out of admiration or was he implying something? Would Brazilians say none of the soccer players add up to anything unless they're Pele? Would Americans say that after Michael Jordon retired, there's no use watching basketball anymore?* I have never been sure if Mamecha's comment was an insult or a compliment. Was this a backhanded compliment, a comment he made to praise Tilahun but also demonize the Oromo tribe? Was his true intent to say that such a tribe is not good enough to produce anything but one singer?

Later, I learned that the *Galla*, or the Oromo tribe as they are known nowadays, were considered by some people to be an inferior tribe. His comment reminded me of my uncle's derogatory comments toward me and other ethnicities in Ethiopia, when he used to insult me with remarks such as, "I wish she [my mother] had had a child with a dog," or "I wish you were dead." "Instead of having you, it would have been better if your mother had kept the placenta." In hindsight, I wonder if perhaps my aunt's husband initially had similar feelings toward me because I was part Arab; perhaps that is why I was made to be a servant in his home.

Shortly after the New Year holiday, my aunt took me to the school she had found for me, which was adjacent to the Imperial Palace. The school had been established for the children of those who were serving at the palace. The students had shoes and were properly dressed, but the class sizes were smaller than those in my school in Nazreth. In Nazreth, the classrooms were bigger, and there were many rooms in a huge complex. The Nazreth school had a soccer field, land for agriculture, and a volleyball court. In Nazreth, I attend classes between grades two and three with students who were much older than me—some of my classmates in grade three were as old as sixteen while I was seven. At my new school, the children were the same age as their classmates; nearly all my grade four classmates were my age.

During those days, some children moved from remote rural locations to cities where more schools were available. Education was considered to be the key or the most critical aspect in life, and everyone was hungry to learn to read and write. Through no fault of their own, the children from more rural areas never were taught in the villages, so when their families flooded the cities and demanded their children be enrolled, the school system didn't have a choice but to accept these children. However, because they were so far behind, the older boys and girls then ended up in lower grades with young children like us simply because of the lack of resources and opportunities where they had come from.

When I had enrolled in school in Nazreth, I was given an entrance exam and based on my results, I was put directly into grade two. Therefore, I would have been in grade five by age ten, as I had skipped a grade. However, I had to lose a year in Nazreth due to living on the streets; I lost what I had gained, as I was unable to attend school for a year.

After I completed one semester of schooling at the Eyou Beliyou (Jubilee Elementary) School, the child who was absent due to a medical condition didn't return to take their seat, so I was able to take that child's place and continue my studies.

*

I continued to perform my house chores, but I didn't like doing them. I felt that the only reasons my aunt had brought me to her home were to assist her with raising her children and to help with the chores. I was doing for free what her male servant had been paid to do, and I started to become resentful.

Often, I thought that I was better off in the street than being stuck in my aunt's house. Yes, there was plenty of food at my aunt's house, clothing to wear, schooling, and acceptable shelter, but I wasn't happy.

Now, at my aunt Emebet's house, the bed-wetting began again. As an adult, I now know that bed-wetting is a sign of trauma. Naturally, my body responded to my feeling unsafe when I was living with my abusive uncle, and now that I was miserable in my aunt's house, it's not surprising that the bed-wetting began again.

Of course, bed-wetting was something my aunt didn't like. She often yelled at me when she saw that I had wet the bed and made me feel that I had something wrong with me.

I didn't respect Mamecha, and I resented my aunt Emebet for essentially making me her slave. I was her nephew; I didn't understand why she was treating me as if I were a servant instead of a family member. I was simply incapable of comprehending what was happening to me and why.

As a form of rebellion, I began neglecting my daily duties and ignoring her expectations of me, which only intensified the conflict between her and me. She often uttered warnings and yelled at me.

Physical and humiliating punishments were highly prevalent in Ethiopia, which had a long and deep-rooted history and a wide social acceptance of corporal punishment for children. My aunt wasn't any different. Whatever she applied to me, she also applied to her own children. That is what she knew.

During my childhood, most adults in Ethiopia considered physical punishment an acceptable means of disciplining children, and while they were against serious and excessive punishments that resulted in physical injury, they were skeptical of official prohibitions and resistant to outside interference. Although most teachers and school staff in principle accepted the total abolition of corporal punishment in schools, they argued against discontinuing this type of discipline because a reasonable alternative for disciplining children was not yet in place. Therefore, they admitted that necessary forms of corporal punishment were regularly being used in schools and homes.

In 2021, when I was doing research for this book, my aunt Emebet reflected on the time I spent living with her and explained her reasons for the harsh punishments she inflicted upon me.

"As a child, you were a hyper, wiry, strong, hasty, and troublesome boy. On the other hand, oddly, no one could compare to your academic skills. You were good at school and always at the top of your class! In particular, your handwriting was impeccable! Ever since you learned how to carry a book, you were inseparable from reading material. Your reading ability, particularly, was unmatched; to you, that was second nature."

She continued, with a bit of hesitation, "You were the most difficult child to raise, though. Simply put, you were an impossible child. In my opinion, it is easier to raise ten children than one of you! I punished you because you were a very difficult boy. I didn't know how to manage you. I brought you from Nazreth to get you proper life and schooling, but you were like a wild cat—so uncontrollable. As a child, you were somehow destructive, and there was no punishment that I didn't inflict upon you."

She continued to reflect on the trouble I caused her. "One time, you ran away from my home. I just lost my temper, so I shackled your legs with a chain to prevent you from running away and went to the church. When I returned home, I found you running around the house—no shackles. When I asked you how you managed to remove the metal chain off your legs, you replied, 'St. Gabriel has freed me.'"

"However, it was because you had been chained for too long and you were physically getting so skinny that the chain slipped off of your ankle."

I had forgotten this incident and couldn't help but laugh as I imagined the scene.

XII

Boys and Girls

One may have two legs, but that does not mean one can climb two trees at the same time.

— Ethiopian proverb

Young Reporter

The following three entries from my childhood journal show the mindset of an eleven-year-old boy who was adjusting to finally having a normal family life.

Journal Entry from January 9, 1973

One Tuesday, on the above indicated date, during late afternoon hours, in the field near our house, while playing "Six Korkes," a children's game, an unexpected accident happened to Getahun [my cousin]. [This game resembles the cricket game.]

This incident has shocked, scared, and frightened the entire family! On that day, Getahun, without eating his snack, decided to put his school notebooks at home, and swiftly left the house to play the game with his friends.

During the game, as he was running in a fast and furious way, he stumbled on a dead tree root. Upon kicking this root, due to his speed and the impact of hitting the root with his foot, he ended up flying about three meters [ten feet] up in the air before falling on the ground. As a result, his face was disfigured beyond recognition.

After the game, when he returned home, his face was swollen badly. His sisters and brother, Meseret, Benyam, and Aynalem (including his whole family), were running away from him. They simply couldn't stomach seeing his disfigured appearance.

In particular, Meseret was so scared and screaming loudly during that evening. When I asked her why she was crying and what she was scared of, she told me that her bother "looks like a monster, and he was going to eat her alive!"

This article was written by Alemayehu.[1]

Journal Entry from April 10, 1973

On this day, it was around 7:30 pm, on Tuesday night, when Alemayehu was asked to bring a eucalyptus tree branch leaf that was used to treat the common cold. The tree branch is also intended to be used on the children [similar to a belt used to punish children].

At that moment, Alemayehu opened the courtyard door to head to the nearest eucalyptus forest. He continued his journey to the local eucalyptus forest, approximately seventy-five meters [eighty-two yards] away from home. Just as a cat saw a squirrel, while looking for the right type of tree, which is an easy way to hit its target, his eyes suddenly fell on a tree that looked like it was only there for its looks. It was a tall and well-groomed tree.

Alemayehu was so happy with its appearance that he decided to climb the tree without any plans. Approximately 2.5 meters [eight feet] up above the ground, while still hanging on the tree, an unexpected event occurred that he didn't see coming. Involuntarily, he was on his way going down to earth. He fell badly. The earth was rotating in his head.

He didn't know where he was and where he was lying. After that incident, he stayed a couple of days sleeping to recover and abstained from roaming around in the neighborhood.

Journal Entry from April 14, 1973

It was Saturday on April 14, 1973. It was also a day before the Easter holiday in Ethiopia. On this day, something interesting happened. Meseret, my cousin, during the evening hours of 10:15 p.m., after floundering around in the kitchen, where our mother and the maids were hustling and bustling, she came to the upper house [the main floor].[2]

At the upper house, there were three people at the time: Getahun, our uncle[3] and me. Getahun and I were watching TV while my uncle was taking a nap. Meseret entered the room where we sat and asked, "Hi guys. Do you need anything?" Getahun asked her if she would hand him something to wear, as he was feeling cold. She refused. Then he turned to me and requested that I give her an order. Which I did and she agreed to do so. She quickly left the room, locking the door behind her. She didn't return with something to wear for Getahun; she didn't come back.

Much later, when she returned to the same room where we were at, she frantically woke our uncle from his sleep. She told him that our mother sent her to inform him of the fact that there is a scream for help, and she wanted him to check. And then she quickly departed the room.

Our uncle jumped from his nap like a fireman and started to check the area. He found nothing. He went to the kitchen, where the ladies clustered, to verify the matter with our mother. Our mother told him that she didn't hear any screaming, nor did she send Meseret to get his attention.

In a typical way, our mother called Meseret's name to inquire how she came up with such a story. Meseret had disappeared and was nowhere to be found. She did not respond to our calls. We all started searching for Meseret's whereabouts. We were unable to find her.

Getahun

Despite being unhappy with my living situation at my aunt's house, I was grateful for one aspect of my life. Getahun, my aunt's oldest son, and I became close friends. Although I have four half brothers on my mother's side, this cousin was my true brother.

He was six years younger than me and followed me everywhere. We played hide and seek, and I helped him with his homework. We remained close in our later years as well. He was the one who brought meals to me when I was held as a political detainee during 1976 and 1977. He too thought of me as his brother rather than his cousin.

As a child, he stole and read my journal. I didn't know about it at the time, but he later told me he did so. Apparently, while I was detained for political reasons, he went through my belongings and found the hidden diary. We bonded more after his admission, as he was the only person to learn how I felt at that time. In fact, he told me he couldn't stop crying while reading about my childhood. Up until that point, he didn't know how much suffering I had endured.

Getahun passed away at a young age in London, UK, leaving behind two boys aged ten and seven. I feel sad that he didn't live long enough to read the story of my life after I left Ethiopia. I don't regret anything in my life except his death.

Soccer

Soccer was and still is a huge part of my life.

As I settled into life at my aunt's house, I expanded my circle of friends, quickly becoming a popular student and playing on the school soccer team. Some of my classmates took advantage of me by getting me to help them with their homework.

Obviously, as a homeless child living on the streets of an Ethiopian city in the early 1970s, I couldn't join a soccer team or club like children in Canada or the US do these days. Even after moving to Addis Ababa to live with my aunt, I stuck to playing soccer informally with friends on the street until I worked my way onto the soccer team at school. The other boys in my neighborhood and I formed our own soccer teams and competed against each other on the streets, in the same way that Canadian boys play street hockey with their friends from the neighborhood. We followed the list of rules below. (During that time, girls didn't play soccer.)

Street Soccer Rules in Ethiopia

These rules are almost universal. In countries on every continent, except for Canada and the US, you can see kids gather on the streets and play according to these rules—the unwritten-(until now)-but-very-strict-and-formal rules for the very-formal-and-extremely-well-organized Ethiopian street soccer league:

1. *The person who owns the ball gets to dictate the rules.*

2. *Let's face it—we are all too poor to own a proper soccer ball, so use whatever is available: car tires, rugs, trash, whatever you can find in the rubbish or on the street. If you have multiple options, choose the most miserable-looking item you can find.*

3. *Same with goal posts. Use whatever is handy: marks on a wall, tree branches, rocks, pieces of garbage.*

4. *If no one owns the "ball," the person who finds or brings an object to use as a ball becomes the "owner" and gets to make the rules.*

5. *Always argue about the rules. Just don't piss off the owner of the ball (see Rule #1)!*

6. *If you do piss off the ball owner, the game is (likely) over. His call, though. Depends on how pissed off he is.*

7. *No shoes. Chances are you don't own shoes anyway, but if you do, wearing them to play soccer is not allowed. If you wear your shoes for playing, you know what will happen when you get home ....*

8. *The best player gets to pick the teams.*

9. *The worst player is the goaltender.*

10. *No minimum or maximum number of players on a team. Just try to make them even.*

11. *No referee. They are just an annoyance, and a useless, extra body taking up space!*

12. *No such thing as offside. Just run as fast as you can when you get the ball!*

13. *Goal tenders don't use gloves. Gloves are for professional clubs or rich kids. Or kids in cold countries.*

14. *The youngest boy has to fetch water for the other players.*

15. *No girls allowed!*

16. *If the ball goes over a wall, the youngest player has to fetch it, so make sure you don't kick the ball over the fence while he is off getting water!*

17. *If the ball damages a neighbor's car or other property, no one knows who kicked it. Ever. What happens in Ethiopian Street Soccer League stays in Ethiopian Street Soccer League.*

18. *No tackling.*

19. *In order for a player to get a penalty, there has to be blood or a broken bone. If the injured player isn't needing a hospital, his injury is just Hollywood.*

20. *If the school bell is about to ring, next goal wins regardless of the score.*

At school, I watched other children playing soccer. Knowing that no one would want to be a goalie because of its low status, I offered to be a goalkeeper so I could get on the team. After a few weeks, I didn't have to wait on the sidelines to be permitted to join the teams; the other children began asking me to man the goal. I gradually managed to get more playing time and was able to impress them with some maneuvers. Often, I alternated positions between goalie, defense, and offense. I became a valuable and versatile team member, playing where and when they needed me.

The same children started to recognize me in the classroom. I was the one who answered the most difficult questions or earned the highest marks on quizzes and exams. Some of the bullies tried to physically intimidate me if I didn't let them cheat from me on exams or assist them with assignments. Most Ethiopians are taller than Yemenis on average. Perhaps also due to my Yemeni blood but also due to my having been born two months premature, malnutrition, and harsh living conditions between the age of five and ten, I have always been petite, and when I was a child, I looked about three years younger than most kids at my age.

Since I've always had a healthy ego and strong self-worth, I have never felt short or inferior. However, others didn't see me the same way I viewed myself. For example, my physical education instructor always put me up front.

Once I asked him, "Why are you putting me in the front of the line?"

He responded, "If I don't put you here in front of me, I won't be able to find you!" as I was also very active and moving consistently. All the kids laughed.

The bullies never did beat me up, but I negotiated money, a better position on the soccer team, or a portion of their snacks. I never let them cheat off of me on exams, but I helped them complete their homework, as no one would know I did it.

I liked helping the girls because I liked their approach and treatment toward me. They started praising my skills and abilities, stroking my ego, and asking how I managed to be so good at schoolwork. The girls always complimented me for beating all the boys in the 100- and 200-meter races. Before I knew it, the girls were pulling out their exercise books and asking how I would solve a math problem or asking for my answer to any academic questions, and I found it impossible to refuse their requests. They were also generous, sharing with me the snacks they brought from their respective homes. Girls never demanded anything of me like the boys would.

However, there was one girl in my class who didn't massage my ego like the other girls did. When teachers were absent, there were no substitute teachers to fill in for them.

Instead, one of the best students would become monitor and tutor for the day. One day, our class was without our teacher, and because I am a nerd and was proud of my academic abilities, I volunteered to be teacher for the day. One of my classmates, a girl who was two or three years older than me, left the class. Because I was so conscientious about schooling and wanted everyone to do well in their classes, I followed her outside, where I found her hanging out under a tree with a boy.

"Why are you skipping the class?" I asked her, once I caught up to her under the tree.

"Who do you think you are?" she replied. "And what are you going to do about it?"

She obviously didn't hold me in the same esteem that the other students did.

"You need to come back to class," I ordered her.

She was having none of it—this runty boy ordering her around as if he were the actual teacher. She stood up, started pushing me, and made it clear she wanted to fight. So like a boxer, I took my position—I assumed the stance and put my hands up in front of my face, fists curled, arms bent in front of me as if I were Mohammed Ali. She couldn't be bothered with proper boxing form. She extended her right arm straight out from her side, pulled it back behind her, wound up, and belted me, knocking me to the ground in one shot. I thought the earth was rotating around me or that there had been an earthquake, and the boy who was with her was laughing so hard.

I got up, dusted myself off, and silently went back to the school building. All of my classmates likely saw all of this happen out of the window. I never asked a student to stay in class after that.

First Crush

The first girl I fell in love with was named Manella Carmelo. There is nothing special about this except that it was my first love. Reflecting on my feelings for her, the only thing that might have caught my attention was her looks; she was different. With her long, flowing dark hair, light skin, and dark, round eyes, she looked Italian. She was 75 percent Italian, as only one of her grandmothers was Ethiopian. Perhaps I sensed she would feel the same way toward me since we both had a mixed parental background. I may have assumed that she could relate to my challenges and predicaments. I didn't know I was in love then and only realized it much later in my life after I became old enough to examine and recognize the different types of feelings that different relationships evoked—the difference in how I liked my cousins or male friends versus being attracted to a girl. In fact, I was happy to realize I had been in love, as I didn't think I would be due to my difficult childhood.

When someone is in love, there is nothing else they can think of. I used to see or imagine her face in the clouds or in the shape of the moon. In school, I did everything I could so that she would notice me. I didn't think I had the looks to be noticed, so my focus was on my achievements just so she would pay attention to me: playing sports, scoring higher grades than the other children, and maintaining a good standing in my social circle. The object of someone's affection can make the afflicted person excel even without acknowledging their existence; wanting the other person's attention is the driving force to try and *get* them to notice. That was my case. I don't think my feelings were reciprocated.

The New Me

When I was still attending elementary school near the Imperial Jubilee Palace, Mamecha purchased a plot of land and started to build a house slightly south of the city. He and my aunt began spending much of their time inspecting the house they were preparing to move to once it was completed.

In September 1973, when I was eleven, Emebet and Mamecha moved to their new house. It was the middle of the semester, and my aunt hadn't yet found me a school near her new place. The distance between her new house and my school was about twelve kilometers (7.5 miles). She agreed that I would continue to attend the same school until she could register me in a new school. Despite the distance, I was happy to be staying at the same school because that meant I could continue to visit with Bansser at the end of the school day.

Later, at the new school she found for me near her house, the structure of the education system was designed to be a three-tier 4-4-4 system (four years each of primary, intermediate, and secondary education). The subjects offered were Amharic, English, science, art, geography, history, arithmetic, music, handicrafts, and physical education. In grades three and four, English was used as the medium of instruction for teaching science, geography, history, and arithmetic. In grades five and six, all subjects except for Amharic were taught in English.

I enrolled in the new intermediate school using the neighbor's son's school certificate. I had two reasons for this choice. First, I didn't want to be called "Adel" because along with my name always came questions I had to answer. My name always brought me unwanted attention as it's not an Ethiopian name. For an Amhara Christian family, my name was a taboo. Registering in a new school where no one knew me gave me a fresh start without those questions or issues. The other reason was logistical; the name change allowed me to easily register for the school.

The neighbor's son's name was Alemayehu Belayneh. Coincidently, my nickname given to me by my mother was Alemayehu, which means, "I saw the world", as in, witnessing prosperity and happiness. Every student had a school certificate for each year that they were enrolled in school, and the neighbor boy took his certificate from the previous year and somehow managed to change his last name to Bezuneh. His name in Amharic is written as follows: አለማየሁ (Alemayehu) በላይነህ (Belayneh). Changing the Amharic characters subtly and slightly allowed the certificate to read ብዙነህ (Bezuneh) instead of በላይነህ (Belayneh). Coincidentally, Bezuneh was my uncle's surname (my mother's brother who was abusive to me), so altering the certificate made it look like I was the son of my uncle Bezuneh, making me a son of siblings (my mother and her brother). But I didn't care, as long as I found a way to attend school.

My aunt didn't know about this plan; if she had, she would have never agreed to it. She did find out later. When the school report came out and my new name was on it, I had to explain the name on the report. She wasn't happy I had made the change, especially without her permission, but she was pleased that I was able to continue going to school and that I consistently achieved good grades.

I liked the idea of starting a new school with a new name, as I didn't want to be called Adel or anything else that would indicate to people that my father was a foreigner with Arab ancestry. I wanted a fresh start, and I didn't want to be ashamed of anything to do with my father's heritage. The name change was liberating. Because of the way my Ethiopian uncle had spoken to and treated me, I knew how the Amhara felt about Arabs.

The downside of enrolling at the new school was that I was now distanced from Bansser. I had to find ways and excuses to visit him without my aunt knowing. Moreover, I had to walk the twelve kilometers (7.5 miles) one way to see him, while hoping he would give me some money to take public transit back to my aunt's house. However, he was my only connection to my father, and so I made the effort to see him as often as I could.

XIII

Shoeshine

Fitting in and belonging are not the same thing. In fact, fitting in is one of the greatest barriers to belonging. Fitting in is about assessing a situation and becoming who you need to be in order to be accepted. Belonging, on the other hand, doesn't require us to change who we are; it requires us to be who we are.

— Brené Brown

Once I realized at the age of eleven that I had a history, a good father, and relatives abroad, my attitude toward my aunt and her family started changing. I sat down with her one evening telling her I was not interested in buying milk, fetching the charcoal to make coffee, or doing any of the house chores.

She didn't know where this was coming from and she looked at me incredulously, asking, "You must be kidding?"

"No," I said. "I'm not interested in being your servant. I am the son of your sister, not someone you picked up from the street."

"Where did you get this idea, and how dare you talk to me like this?!" she exclaimed.

"It doesn't matter," I said. "I don't want to get the milk tomorrow morning."

At that, she pulled the belt out of her husband's trousers and started belting me. I didn't cry, and I didn't resist; rather I walked away, and I didn't come back home that evening.

I walked to a place called the Police Garage, a local workshop where police cars were taken for repairs and maintenance. The father of a boy I knew worked at the garage, and the boy, Hassan, was working in the community as a shoeshine. I managed to get to the garage just before 6 p.m. and I asked my friend's father if I could speak to Hassan.

The father informed me, "He's out working, and you can go and find him."

I proceeded to the workshop area and started looking for Hassan. He was Muslim and was from an ethnic group called *Gurage*. The Gurage people are Habesha people (Semitic language speakers) inhabiting Ethiopia. They traditionally inhabit a fertile, semi-mountainous region in central Ethiopia, about 125 kilometers (seventy-eight miles) southwest of Addis Ababa, bordering the Awash River in the north; the Gibe River, a tributary of the Omo River, to the southwest; and Lake Zway in the east.[1]

I waited until Hassan finished his work at hand, and I spoke to him about my situation.

"What are you going to do?" he asked me.

"My aunt is not treating me very well. She thinks I am her servant and that I'm only there to serve her. She also beat me up today. I'm not planning to return to her home."

He asked me again, "What you are going to do?"

I answered him, "I need to work with you, and I want to be a shoeshine like you every afternoon after school."

"That would be hard for you because you don't know how to do that," he told me.

Since he was a member of the Gurage ethnic group, his Amharic was weak.

I assured him, "I'll try. In fact, you don't speak good Amharic, and I can speak good Amharic and bring you more customers. We can work together that way."

He went silent, pondering my proposition, and finally he said, "Let me think about it."

"I'm not going to go home. Is there a way I can spend the night at your place?"

"That's not possible," he told me. "We only have one room. My dad and I sleep in a very small shop not bigger than two meters [6.5 feet]. There is no space, to be honest."[2]

"Is there anything you can do to help me?" I asked.

"I can give you a bedsheet and you can sleep over there," he offered.

He pointed out to me a brand-new concrete sewer system that was across the street from his father's shop.

His suggestion sounded good to me.

"Okay," he said. "You go inside, and I'll cover you with cardboard boxes. Cover yourself with the blanket and the bedsheet and spend the night there. In the morning, I'll come and get you before you go to school."

He gave me an old shoeshine box he had used in the past. We agreed to work together and split the profits.

We walked together to the back of his father's shop and across the street to a tiny booth—the new septic system he had pointed out to me. He had grabbed a bedsheet and cardboard box out of his father's shop and brought it, and I jumped inside the cistern.

He covered the top of the concrete circle with the cardboard and said to me, "Goodnight. See you tomorrow."

I had trouble getting to sleep. I don't remember when I finally fell asleep, but I do remember lying awake hearing drunk individuals from a nearby bar walking by, and in the morning, I heard the sound of motor vehicles.

I woke to the sound of someone calling my name. It was Hassan, and he asked me to get up.

"Okay," I said.

It was daylight. I struggled to jump over the concrete.

"We can't leave the bedsheet and cardboard box here with this concrete. We must take it back to my dad's. Drop it there in his shop before you go to school," Hassan pointed across the street to his father's shop.

After an uncomfortable and noisy night sleeping in the concrete sewer system, I was tired, and the past week had been a traumatic week for me what with fighting with my aunt, and having to again sleep on the street. After leaving the bedsheet and cardboard box at Hassan's father's shop, I dragged myself off to school. Hassan walked with me.

Why didn't I stop attending school? I think that was the only place I felt worthy. School was the place I could show that I was better than others—far better than most children—academically.

Later that day, after school, Hassan and I went back to his father's shop, and I began my apprenticeship.

For some reason, he gave me only a small amount of polish. I suspect it was because if I ever disappeared, at least I wouldn't have run away with a good portion of the polish he had in his possession. The polish was a huge capital investment for him. I didn't have any intention of stealing from him, though. In fact, I really liked him, and I appreciated his support. That afternoon, I carefully watched how Hassan performed his shoeshine duties and tried to learn from him.

After about an hour, I felt I was ready. I was so excited, and I said, "I am eager to take on the next customer."

We waited but nobody showed up. As we sat in the shoeshine box, he started asking me questions about my name.

"Are you a Muslim?"

I told him I was an Arab.

He said, "All Arabs are Muslims."

"I don't know. I heard my father celebrated Christmas," I replied.

"Are you sure?" he asked.

"Yeah, that's what they told me."

"I read and studied the Qur'an for a couple of years," I added.

Next, he asked me about my mother.

"I don't know where my mother is. I'll find out."

Why did I tell him this? I had never worried much about my mother in the past. Most likely my stepmother had filled the gap while my father was alive. Since I didn't have any memory of my biological mother, I don't think I had the urge to think or ask about her.

Right then, a few police officers jumped off of their motorbikes and one of them called out, "*Listro!*" (shoeshine).[3]

I didn't know what language the police officer was speaking. It was new to me. Hassan responded to the man, and I ran over to the officer with Hassan. I started talking to the officer and asked him if I could give him a one cent discount. Hassan went silent. I sat down to start polishing this man's shoes, but I didn't realize how clumsy I was. This officer noticed that I wasn't good and that I didn't know what I was doing.

"No wonder your price is low!" he grumbled.

He pulled his shoe away from me and told me to get lost. Hassan took over.

*

The next day, I approached the bar that was across the street from Hassan's father's workshop—the pub where I had heard drinkers late into the night on the first night I slept in the empty concrete barrel—and asked the owner if I could spend the night there. He asked why and inquired as to where my parents were. I told him they were both dead.

He agreed, but he told me there were conditions.

"What are the conditions?" I asked.

"At midnight, after all the customers have left, you must fold the chairs and clean the floor," he elaborated.

I agreed.

For the next two to three weeks, my rituals were to get up and go to school, work as a shoeshine boy after school, go to the bar to watch TV with a bunch of adults (half of them were always drunk), clean the place, and then go to sleep in the bar once the patrons left.

Every other day, I spent a good portion of my day at Bansser's dry-cleaning shop, Zenith. He allowed me to take orders, issue receipts, and even handle cash transactions. At the end of each day, when I was about to leave the laundry, he gave me a *birr*[4] or two, which meant I didn't have to work as a shoeshine boy for long. Instead, I just went to the garage to hang around with Hassan and get ready for bed at the bar.

I didn't tell Bansser that I was a runaway child, nor did I tell him about my problems with my aunt. I just enjoyed hanging out at Zenith and listening to his stories about my father. He seemed to laugh whenever he remembered details about my father. When I pressed him to tell me the stories in more detail, he withheld some information and promised to tell me more once I got older, at least fifteen. I kind of suspected those stories involved adult topics, so I let it go.

Whenever I saw him grinning and about to say something but didn't, I wanted to know more about what he was thinking. In fact, I started to be way too curious about what he *didn't* say.

I began to get the impression my father was a mischievous and adventurous man—that he was a player, a bully, and a commanding force. Through what Bansser told me, but also because of what he *didn't* tell me, I started to create a more thorough image of my father. I continually asked Bansser questions, mostly to fill the gaps in my mind. "Was my father was like this?" "Would my father accept or reject this?" "What did my father say about this or that?"

It was like putting a puzzle together. Often, I wondered if Bansser was telling me the whole truth or not, and I frequently asked the same questions to see if there were any inconsistencies in his stories and to validate if what he told me was true.

Bansser was always happy to entertain my questions. He never tired of responding to my inquires, nor did he ask why I had so many questions.

I knew the details he omitted were about my father's bad habits, as he was selective to eliminate adult topics like my father's womanizing or his drinking. As I got older, though, Bansser slowly and selectively start to share with me the full picture of my father and his improprieties. Regardless of my father's faults, Bansser's respect and admiration for my father remained unwavering.

Whenever he had time, he drove me to other Hadhrami families to introduce me. Mostly we went to their shops and offices, and occasionally we went to pay his condolences for someone who had passed away. As a result of these visits, I came to know the Baobaid, Ben-Salem, Baquehum, Bazara, and Baharon families, and more—people who would, over time, become significant influences and mentors for me. The strange part was that other than Bagarsh's son Abubaker, and Baqehum's son Awadh (Awadh Baqehum is a former

Ethiopian national team soccer player), I hardly met or mingled with any of the children in these families.

Why? This is a question I am unable to answer. I must admit, when I was living in North Yemen, most other *Muwalladin*[5] kept asking me, "How come we never saw you in Addis Ababa or were aware of you?" I simply didn't have an answer at the time.

Today, reflecting on this topic, the only rationale I am able to come up with is … perhaps shame. To be born out of wedlock in Islam is a sin. Also, I had enough problems explaining who I was to Ethiopian children and didn't want another group of children asking me about my mother's story. They probably never cared or asked, but I felt shame due to my uncle's insults. I was ashamed to be called an Arab. To be thought of as a bastard, to be considered unfit by all parties … avoidance was perhaps the best remedy.

*

My aunt came to school to find out what was going on as she hadn't seen me in several weeks. The school principal checked my attendance and informed her that there was no absenteeism in my records. My aunt was perplexed as to where I was spending the nights and how I was feeding myself. She stalked me and managed to find and capture me at the gate of the school grounds just as I was leaving the property. She grabbed me by the ears and kept pulling and twisting my ears and screaming at me until I submitted to her.

"Where have you been this whole time?" she shrieked at me.

It had been almost four weeks since I had run away. I struggled, trying to break away from her, but she made sure I didn't get loose. She dragged me home by my ear.

Once we arrived at her home, she gave me a stern warning about what I did and what the consequences would be if I ever ran away again. She was angry that I had run away, but she was also ashamed that I had been working as a shoeshine boy. Her husband ran a successful business, and for me to be a shoeshine was degrading. My actions would have embarrassed her and made it look to the community like she wasn't adequately supporting me.

She sat me down, and we proceeded to have what was probably the first real and honest conversation she and I had had with each other since she had retrieved me from Nazreth. She listened to me complain about her treatment of me, and gradually her look become one more of concern and hopelessness than anger.

I knew she was vulnerable from the tone of her voice. She proceeded to tell me the main reason she made me do house chores was that it was a condition her husband had put in place if I was to live at their house. Making that agreement with him was the only way she could have secured shelter for me at her home. It made some sense to me, and my anger subsided.

She continued and repeated, "I have no means to support you, and your mother is not in a position to assist you. We didn't know how to reach your family in South Yemen. The only way I could manage to bring you from Nazreth was by promising my husband you would help around the house."

She emphasized to me that she hadn't had any choice but to negotiate with her husband the conditions he put on keeping me safe and off the streets.

It became clear to me that day that an Ethiopian woman did not have a safety net. I sensed she wanted to me understand the hoops she had to go to keep me off the street.

She asked me, "Do you understand?"

I said, "Yes, but …."

"But what?" she demanded to know.

Then I told her, "I was happier on the street than at your house."

Then I saw tears in her eyes.

"Explain it. Why?" she wanted to know. "I'm feeding you; I bought you shoes and clothes, put you in school. Most children with parents don't get two meals a day. What else do you want?" She demanded an answer.

Then I told her, "I feel I moved from survival mode to slavery mode. You don't treat me as a family member. You treat me as if I'm only a servant boy."

She put her head down. We both went quite for a couple of minutes.

Finally, she said, "If you choose to go and be on street, it is your choice. I can only do what I can to keep you safe," and with that, she left the room.

I never ran away again.

Although, I didn't know anything about women's rights at the time, ever since that moment, it was clear to me that

157

women in Ethiopia had limited influence. I finally understood that my mother was unable to take me due to her husband being unwilling to accommodate me. And I recognized that my aunt had had to negotiate a living arrangement to rescue me. If it had been who Mamecha had found me, and I was his blood relative, there would have been no discussion with my aunt about bringing me home; he simply would have done so. It was a man's world!

This realization was a turning point in my understanding of my own cultures. In Ethiopia, and in the Arab world, everyone asks who your father is; no one asks about your mother. Not having a father is shameful. Therefore, I was at a disadvantage, and I felt less than because I came from the female side of the family. And my mother and aunt had no choice but to abide by their husbands' decisions.

That conversation was a turning point for all of us. Her husband became a kinder, more generous person. He grew to respect me and I him. We came to the agreement that from then, if I helped his children with their schoolwork, he would care less about the rest of my duties. In fact, he was pleased and was proud of me for all of my school achievements. Over time, I found him to be a gentle soul, much more so than my uncle was. And he never insulted me based on my ethnicity.

XIV

Religion and a Child

The world of religion isn't a logical world; that's why children like it. It's a world of worked-out fantasies, very similar to children's stories or fairy tales.

— Yehuda Amichai

Having read the three Holy Books of the Qur'an, Old Testament (Hebrew Bible), and New Testament (Christian Bible) a few times before the age of thirteen, I came to understand the foundations of Judaism, Christianity, and Islam to basically be the same. Clearly, God didn't appear to have a religion and all the dressings, at least in my mind. Moreover, at a young age, I noticed multiple personal flaws and hypocrisies in the religion teachers I had to deal with. However, despite finding the religious texts boring overall, I did enjoy the individual stories in these books and accepted them. I also respected the core values all of the books teach.

The Qur'an is written in Arabic and read from right to left. Although I could count numbers and write simple sentences at a grade four or five level in Arabic by the age of fourteen, understanding the Qur'an was an uphill battle. We were expected to memorize the verses, but we always had the teacher interpret the words and phrases for us if we needed help understanding verses. The entire Qur'an is supposed to be memorized, and the melody is beautiful to hear when someone is reciting its verses, but memorization doesn't guarantee comprehension.

The Hebrew Bible was in the Amharic alphabet, but the language wasn't in Amharic; it was in Geʿez. I could only understand a word or two in every sentence. Aha. I finally understood the method to Gideon's madness—why he insisted on teaching me Geʿez. Turns out he was the expert after all! Again, because I didn't fully understand the written Geʿez, the teacher had to interpret the stories and the law of Moses and all the prophets.

The New Testament was written in Amharic, and it was easier for me to comprehend, perhaps because I was much older (thirteen), when I started to attend Sunday school at an evangelical bible school—Precious Seed International church—with my friend Matias. I had to refresh my knowledge of the New Testament again in my early twenties when I was living with a Mormon family in the US. The Book of Mormon, which was born in North America, is perhaps the newest of all of the religious books I have studied throughout my life.

Family members on both my mother's and my father's sides were devout to their religions and insisted their version of the Holy Book was the holiest and the purest. But despite being from Coptic Christian origins, none of my mother's side of the family ever sat me down to teach me Christianity. Largely, most of them do not read the Holy Book due to low levels of literacy.

I didn't—and still don't—see any difference between any of the religions as all the books teach love, respect, kindness, and support for each other. I also didn't like the forceful approach of teaching or dealing with a child and the regimens required to follow specific rituals.

For example, my Arabic teacher had taught me that the Prophet Muhammed (pbuh) was once sitting with a child in his lap, and the child urinated over the Prophet Muhammed (pbuh). Embarrassed, the father scolded the child. But the Prophet Muhammed (pbuh) restrained the father and advised him, "This is not a big issue. My clothes can be washed. But be careful with how you treat the child. What can restore his self-esteem after you have dealt with him in public like this?" As a young teenager, I felt that the Prophet Mohammed's (pbuh) approach displayed a much more reasonable and humane response than the corporal punishment I had endured up to that point.

The Prophet Muhammed (pbuh) also showed love to children of other religions, as exemplified when he once visited his Jewish neighbor's son when the child was sick.

A parent or guardian is responsible for teaching their children according to Islam as follows:

- *basic information about belief and worship*

- *basic information about high moral qualities*

- *information on what to be careful about in relations with other people*

- *vocational education*

The actual practice of those teachings was totally different in the people around me when I was growing up. Everyone operated by using fear and guilt to intimidate and control children, and punishment was often in the form of beatings.

Being forced to get up as early as 5 a.m. for dawn prayer (*Fajr*) is one of the worst memories I have from my childhood. I just never understood why a child had to be up that early to pray. What sin did I commit to deserve such punishment? I wanted to sleep!

And then there was the requirement of fasting during the month of Ramadan. My resistance to fasting was for a couple of reasons. Regardless of the issue at hand, I have just never responded well to forced structure or discipline. I operate better if I'm convinced with the notion—if I've bought into something rather than being manipulated or forced. (Maybe a psychologist would enjoy diagnosing me. If someone tells me to do something, I will do the opposite because I am stubborn!)

Additionally, between the ages of eight and ten, I rarely found a meal a day. Often, I would go days without eating because of my circumstances. Even if I ate once a day, my so-called meal was never more than a piece of bread, or if I were lucky or quick enough, a loaf of bread or handful potatoes that I stole, or that was given to me by Ms. Abebech. I knew well what hunger felt like. I knew first-hand what it was like to have nothing. Therefore, I didn't want to fast to prove my faith to anyone. I had already been forced to fast due to my circumstances and perhaps would continue to do so until my living conditions improved. I concluded that fasting should be done by those who are rich and in possession of excess food—those who have little knowledge of what it means to have nothing. Although I respected the principles of fasting, I simply didn't think they should apply to me.

Fasting, one of the Five Pillars or duties of Islam, is meant to remind Muslims of those who are less fortunate and to reinforce the need to be thankful. Adults are required to fast during the month of Ramadan. The only adults who are exempt are the elderly, those who are physically or mentally incapable of fasting, pregnant women, breastfeeding mothers, and travelers. Children who have not yet reached puberty are also exempt.[1] However, I was asked to fast as early as the age of eight, and I was resentful. I thought, *I'm already poor and don't need to be reminded how to be poor.*

My other argument against fasting is this: I am only half Arab! I was born to a Coptic Christian mother, and therefore, I should only be required to fast 50 percent of the time, at most!

Despite all the preaching and convincing arguments that were passed on to me, I was never able to accept those two conditions: prayers at dawn and fasting. From the get-go, as a child, I felt like a misfit who was ill-prepared to be a good Muslim. Just like a birth defect! Perhaps I truly was my father's son ....

On the other hand, I admired and appreciated the generosity of the Islamic religion. In particular, the *zakat* (alms) dictate that Muslims happily give to those who are less fortunate. The impressive part of zakat is that the receiver doesn't know who has given the charity, as it is done anonymously. Although I wasn't clear on the context of discrimination at the time, according to the teachings of the Prophet Muhammed (pbuh), skin color, ethnicity, age, gender, etc. are not contributing factors to viewing another human as lesser or higher. All are equal in Islam. I fondly remember and cherish the money I received as a child on Eid,[2] after fasting during the month of Ramadan. Of course, even though I wasn't told where it came from, I was fairly certain that the money I was receiving from Bansser must have been from him, Bagarsh, and Baobaid; there was no one else in my life who would have been generously giving me money for Islamic holidays at that time.

Overall, I felt all aspects in each of the religions were based on guilt and fear. Always focused on the rituals and the don'ts. I only wanted to read the stories about miracles and such. In Ethiopia, most families hung pictures of the Virgin Mary with her son, Jesus, on their walls. The image in the pictures depicted a white lady with a reddish-blond child. Every time I stepped into an Ethiopian Orthodox Church, I saw the walls were painted with all kinds of images including The Last Supper. Again, all people in the paintings seemed to be white people. I felt that Christianity was a product of white people and was intended for white people. I didn't feel any connection to Christianity.

I skeptically accepted some of the stories as they seemed old, and they were entertaining and taught good lessons. Although I didn't have the justification for or reasons to push back against the rest of the teachings, I simply never bought into them. I gravitated more toward religious holidays than the theology taught in the books. The Ethiopian holidays are colorful and joyful.

Ethiopian Holidays

My favorite Ethiopian Coptic Christian holidays are Ethiopian New Year (*Enkutatash*, September 11), Ethiopian Christmas (*Genna*, January 7), the commemoration of the baptism of Jesus (*Timket*, January 19 or 20), Easter (*Fasika*, April or May; the date varies), and Finding of the True Cross (*Meskel*, September 26 and 27). The top of my list is Enkutatash, the Ethiopian New Year!

> *Enkutatash means the "gift of jewels." According to legend, the Queen of Sheba returned from her famous visit to King Solomon of Jerusalem some 3,000 years ago with jewels gifted by her host. Her return to Ethiopia after receiving this gift coincided with the New Year celebration in September, and hence the name Enkutatash came to be.[3]*

Enkutatash is when groups of young Ethiopian girls go around performing a song called "Abebayehosh." They carry and hand out bright-yellow flowers, which grow between September and November, to people in the neighborhoods. As a token of appreciation, families give the girls money or bread that is specially prepared for the holidays. The boys tend to bring and distribute drawings of flowers.

September is the end of the rainy season in Ethiopia. It is when the days are sunny, the weather is comfortable, and flowers are blooming, all of which signal the beginning of a new year. The sunnier weather represents happier, brighter days after the rain and fog.[4] Therefore, flowers, as a symbol of spring and new growth, are a significant part of the celebrations.

I was never interested in roaming around the neighborhood to hand out drawings, nor was I allowed to do so, anyway. However, I made money by producing identical drawings to those that were being distributed. Even though I didn't think I had any artistic talent, the boys and girls in the neighborhood thought I had ability and for my efforts, gave me a portion of the money they collected.

My second favorite holiday is *Genna* (Christmas), which is on January 7, the day after my birthday. In fact, I was born on Christmas Eve, or Ethiopian Epiphany! In light of the fact I was born two months premature, I guess I must have been wanting to share a birthday with Jesus!

The third holiday, *Timket* (January 19 or in leap years, January 20), is only a couple of weeks later in the same month. Timket is an Orthodox Christian occasion to mark the baptism of Jesus Christ in the River Jordan, and the celebration lasts three days. On this day, wooden models of the Ark of the Covenant are taken from churches and wrapped in silk. A procession proceeds to the river or public bath, with each church's senior priest carrying on his head replicas of the tablets on which the Ten Commandments were written and presented to Moses by God on Mount Sinai.[5] The priests and some other participants keep vigil over the tablets during the night.

XV

Bibliophile

When the missionaries came to Africa, they had the Bible and we had the land. They said "Let us pray." We closed our eyes. When we opened them, we had the Bible and they had the land.

— Desmond Tutu

In the neighborhood not too far from my aunt's new house, an evangelical bible school and church opened when I was twelve. The church was actively recruiting young children. Now, after nearly fifty years, I was able to trace the founding of this church. It is called Precious Seed International, based in the UK.

Matias, who was one of my elementary school classmates and childhood friends, and I decided to start attending their Sunday services. Matias had apparently already attended their services a couple of times before I started going, and he had been given school supplies. He told me that they would give me notepads and pencils or pens. Sometimes they also handed out shirts and Wrangler jeans.

Because it was common for Ethiopians to insult and discriminate against Arabs, I didn't want Matais (who was Ethiopian) to know that I was half Arab, but I thought getting free school supplies would be a good idea. I could then keep the money my aunt gave me to purchase school supplies and use it to commute to Bansser's laundry from my aunt's new house. With the increased distance, I needed to take a bus to see him.

I attended Precious Seed International with Matias for about nine months and accumulated enough free school supplies for my last few years of school. I even had enough that I started selling or giving away some notebooks and pencils to many poor children.

The teachers at the church were white, but I didn't know which European countries they had come from. I was impressed by their Amharic language skills, but there were several questions in my mind. Ethiopia is one of the oldest nations on this planet, with its own alphabet, language, and calendar, and it was independent. I had been taught that Ethiopia had been a Christian country for 2,000 years, so I didn't understand why Europeans were coming to Ethiopia for the purpose of teaching Christianity. *Why are white people making the effort to teach us what we have already known for centuries?*

I wasn't sure how this new religion would fit into my current life. I didn't see the need to convert to a different version of Christianity (evangelical versus orthodox), and I didn't understand the concept or purpose of missionary work and conversion.

*

When I was fourteen, I asked myself, "Why did the missionaries come to Ethiopia?" They told us they wanted to teach the Ethiopians how to read and write and, in the process, we might understand the words of God.

However, from the teachings of Gideon, I had learned that Judaism existed for several thousand years prior. Ditto for the Ge'ez or Ethiopic script, which possibly developed from the Sabaean script. The earliest known inscriptions in the Ge'ez script date to the fifth century BC. And as per Basherahil, my Islamic school teacher, Islam was in play for over 1,300 years. According to my readings, Christianity came to Ethiopia only seven years after Jesus's birth, making it over 2,000 old in the country. Ethiopians or the East Africans, in general, were never pagans.

Did the influx of missionaries have anything to do with the slave trade combined with predatory capitalism seeking resources for greedy intentions? This is a question I still ask myself; I don't know my answer.

Matias

In 2021, when I was writing this book, I reached out to Matias, who's currently living in the US, to reflect on our childhood days, the church, and related stuff. He wrote me back the following letter and granted me permission to include it in the book:

Hi Adel,

I hope everything is going well and you are surviving, as we all are, the current pandemic safe and sound! I really enjoy the fact that you're attempting to write about yourself, and it's going to be a rich historical perspective for any of our timers.

With that said, I would like to contribute, as follows, to nudge your memories:

Yes, indeed we were so close during our time in Eyou Beliyou Elementary School, especially when it came to our lunch time. I remember, not sure if you recall, there were two brothers whose mom used to work in the Bete Mengist[1] and brought some lunch that we used to scramble to get a bite of. In addition, I remember the time we spent playing soccer, as it's called in the US. And also these were the times spent playing biy and teter,[2] and yes, I used to collect quite a good number of marbles.

Indeed, these were also times that we used to attend the Sunday school of Pentecostal studies. We used to go on Sundays to the biblical studies, and on occasion we used to go to the residence of Mr. McLane (I believe that was his name), which was in Kebele 46, just across from the school.[3] I do not recall what actual denomination they were in except that it was Pentecostal. I do believe we outgrew the Sunday school as we got older and started on the new path to the consciousness.

I also remember that you were involved so much in the timely revolutionary ideas[4] that you and others were imprisoned multiple times. I was the only guy I remember from our circle of friends who was left alone and never got to see the door of imprisonment. I am indebted to you though as you were my mentor in training me on [the] words of Marxism-Leninism and public speaking.

With your encouragement I was able to deliver my first teaching of Marxism-Leninism to a group of people.

We also started playing for the Kebele soccer team right around this time. And as I recall, you were very flexible and strong in that category, which made you fit for the goalie position. I believe you remember the time we had with Gashe Mulugeta[5] in the early morning run we used to do before the sunrise and soccer practice, as well. These were the good times that we had at Kebele playing soccer. Soon after, we heard that you left for North Yemen.

Right after that, the scholarship came around about myself going to Cuba. And voila ... I set off to Cuba for higher education. Luckily, I was able to land in the engineering faculty of my choice to become a professional in electrical engineering specializing in telecommunications. At the age of twenty-three, I became the first one from my family of ten brothers and sisters, in addition to myself, to graduate with a MSc degree in telecommunications engineering in 1985. Soon after settling down in Ethio-Telecom, I started searching for you, my good friend from childhood who was in the US, according to one of my family members. I located you with ease from the free international calls that were available to me as a member of the Ethio-Telecom international switch engineers. I was in contact with you for some time, and we lost contact later before I proceeded to the training I came for at USTTI.[6] Already my girlfriend was in the US. I got the sponsorship of my employer, Qualcomm, and was therefore able to remain in the US. Later on, we settled in San Diego and formed our family of four. Two kids with the names of Ruth Matias and Amanuel Matias. Just the way we are named, they took my first name as their last name. My daughter studied broadcasting and electronic media arts in SFSU[7] and graduated last year. Her younger brother is graduating in mechanical engineering in the coming summer this year. He is going to Connecticut to work as an engineer in the surgical department of Medtronic, a job he secured during an internship this last year. My daughter is currently working as a freelance video editor from home.

Thanks,

Matias Abebe

Alemayehu

After around eight or ten months, I had had enough of religious talks and studies, and I stopped going to the church. For some strange reason, I have always thought of religion as an over-embellished fairy tale. I love to read, and when I was a child, I used to read a book per week. Some of the novels I read at that time were as impressive as the Bible or Qur'an. The difference was that the religious books and stories were forced on me.

Alemayehu, the neighborhood boy who forged a certificate to enroll me in junior high school, had also introduced me to a book club he belonged to, which I eagerly joined.

Belaye, Alemayehu's father, was a retired member of the Ethiopian Imperial Guard (*Kebur Zabagna*—honorable guard).[8] "Also known as the First Division, this unit served the dual purposes of providing security for the Emperor of Ethiopia and being an elite infantry division. It was not, however, part of the organizational structure of the Ethiopian regular army."[9]

Belaye never accepted no as an answer. He reportedly was the best target shooter in his division and one of the best in the country. He was also a well-decorated soldier who had served in the Korean war and was proficient with weaponry. In the later days of his service, he served in the military storage division, where he was known to have befriended the father of Mengistu Haile Mariam, the communist leader who ruled Ethiopia between 1977 and 1991.

Belaye's expectations of his sons were high, both academically and fitness-wise. Therefore, Alemayehu needed to be good at everything and was kept under an extreme regimen. In return, Alemayehu tried to impose those expectations on me and his younger brother, Lamma. We needed to be at the top of the class, come in first in any sports competition or debates, and possess a greater awareness of international affairs than our classmates. We could lose a ping-pong match to each other but not to anyone else. We played volleyball and basketball, despite our height. He never cared how short I was as long as I could compensate with agility and speed during the basketball and volleyball games. Ditto for soccer.

We didn't have guns, but we used slingshots to kill birds and practice our aim in distance shooting for target practice. Over time, our shooting wasn't about killing a bird. Rather, our goal was to reduce how many stones we used to achieve the objective.

"Slingshots can be a lot of fun and can even be a great way to practice bowhunting skills," he would say.

We learned how to use the slingshot with proper form to avoid causing damage or injuries. We considered the slingshot a weapon, so we always used it with caution.

Alemayehu organized a competition something like a mini-Olympics in our neighborhood at one point, with events such as running, jumping, boxing, etc. If I or Lamma failed to win a local track race or earned less than a 95 percent average in any subject in school, he made sure we paid the price. The price ranged between sidebar comments on how sassy or girlish we were or some sort of physical abuse. If he saw a kick in a movie, he made sure he practiced it on us. He was integral in getting me to expand my interests beyond academics to include athletics.

He also had leadership qualities, which he used to give us a huge sense of self-confidence. He didn't care who the opponents were; he always believed we could win.

Alemayehu always said, "There are many huge animals in the jungle—animals that are bigger than the lion—but the king of the jungle is always a lion, not an elephant or giraffe."

He pushed me to read more and more. He was fascinated with anything from electricity to landing on the moon. On all school science projects, we worked together and went above and beyond what the instructors asked for. He mandated that we be able to read at least five hundred words per minute and summarize an entire book in one page.

Due to my early childhood experiences, unhappy life circumstances, and lack of emotional connection to anyone, I gravitated toward his expectation and demands. I immersed myself in books day in and day out.

By my early- to mid-teens, I had read non-fiction books on WW II, Hitler, Mussolini, Gandhi, Kennedy, Churchill, Rommel, G. Montgomery, Socrates, Aristotle, and other historic figures and events. I thought reading and citing religious books was the most boring thing to do, as the value didn't equate for me, but I was fascinated with history and philosophy.

And my way of expressing my frustration and anger toward life, my relatives, and lack of belonging was writing. I continued to write in my journals.

XVI

Revolution

Above all, try always to be able to feel deeply any injustice committed against any person in any part of the world. It is the most beautiful quality of a revolutionary.

— Che Guevara

*C*hange is necessary! However, radical change, whether it be to an individual or a whole society, can often result in unintended and undesired outcomes.

Given my limited understanding of Ethiopia's history, its social fabric, and its diverse ethnic composition, looking back, I would say reform was necessary. The archaic, autocratic, and monarchial rule required modification to realign society and hierarchies and address the many questions with regards to regions, faith, and ethnic groups. However, in spite of this need for change, the violent and radical political drama of the 1970s was uncalled for.

In my early teens, I read every revolutionary book that was available to me and learned the ideologies, mainly imported from abroad, that the youth at that time thought were a way out of poverty. The results of the political upheaval in Ethiopia at that time were mass migration, brain drain, countless killings, and kidnappings, all of which left the land in huge financial ruin and somewhat ethnically divided. In my opinion, the revolution pushed the county backward into its weakest condition in its history.

From a personal perspective, the revolution did solidify my identity and connect me back to my father's side of my heritage, eventually pushing me to leave Ethiopia at a young age. Without such unprecedented events, most children born in Ethiopia who had Yemeni origins wouldn't have considered departing their place of birth. The events of the mid- to late-70s finally opened the door for me and countless others to move to North Yemen, as I had hoped to do at the time of my father's death years earlier.

The Student Movement

In 1974, when the Ethiopian Revolution and related movements started, I completed grade six at the top of my class with a 96 percent score on provisional exams. I was a class representative and held tutorial sessions when teachers didn't show up for a class. I befriended a bunch of boys in the neighborhood and played in a local soccer club, and I was in a book club. I was finally a normal kid.

Some of the youth I socialized with as part of the book club were much older than me. For example, when I was fourteen, I had friends in their early- or mid-twenties. The age differences were irrelevant, though, because the connection I had with the older individuals was at an intellectual level. I was eager to learn, read well, and provide satisfying analysis; therefore, my tender age and petite physical stature were not factors. I was proud to be at the same intellectual level as young adults. On the other side, members of the youth socialist movement were dazzled to find a young boy who was knowledgeable of and able to talk about most topics their peers were unable to. They called me "Chu Che": "the kid" or "kiddo."

The country was going through a shock. While the adults were trying to comprehend what was happening, the youth were hyped about the changes on the horizon. My aunt had a black-and-white National-branded TV. She and her husband, along with other adult neighbors who didn't have a TV set in their homes, clustered around and glued themselves to the TV at our house to watch the news showing the uprisings and demonstrations. It was a traumatic and confusing time, but I gravitated toward knowing more about it and continued to read newspapers and everything else I could find, including several books on the history of Ethiopia. Even though I was a twelve-year-old, I knew that what was happening was different—and monumental.

*

In 1960, before I was born, an attempted coup d'état had taken place on December 13. In the 1970s, it was fresh in the minds of many adults, and I couldn't help hearing about it. The older generations were comparing the past event with the current movements.

> *The Council of the Revolution, four conspirators led by brothers Germame Neway and Brigadier General Mengistu Neway, commander of the Kebur Zabangna (Imperial Bodyguard), sought to overthrow Emperor*

Haile Selassie during a state visit to Brazil in order to install a progressive government. The coup leaders declared the beginning of a new government under the rule of Haile Selassie's eldest son, Crown Prince Asfaw Wossen, that would address the numerous economic and social problems Ethiopia faced. The Council gained control of most of the capital city, Addis Ababa, and took several ministers and other important people hostage. After its initial success, the majority of the military and populace quickly aligned against the coup, and by 17 December, loyalists had regained control of Addis Ababa. At least 300 people were killed during the coup, including most of the conspirators.[1]

Had that coup been successful, there would have been no need for the extreme revolution of the 1970s. Reform would have taken place gradually. But the coup failed and as a result, tensions built over the years until they exploded into revolution.

Apparently, since the coup, fourteen years of efforts to reform the country had achieved little progress despite all attempts made by the king. Civilians, significant segments of the military, and the police joined the demands for higher pay. Protests in the streets erupted over water rations, the inadequacy of food, changes to fuel prices, the lowering of the pay of government employees, and the reduction of financial support for education.

While a provisional military administrative council formed and began mandating capital punishment for political offenses against it, some students and members of the labor union confederation protested and overturned the Ethiopian government. On November 28, 1974, two former prime ministers and more than fifty other political prisoners were executed. That day became known as Bloody Saturday. Just before the year was out, on December 25, 1974, the new military government issued a proclamation of Ethiopian socialism.

In 1975, when I was thirteen, the older youths in my neck of the woods were quickly enlisted to be members of the Ethiopian People's Revolutionary Party (EPRP), a Marxist-Leninist group. These were the youth who were part of the book club I was in and with whom I played soccer. Due to my connection with them and my voracity for reading about history and culture, I urged them to continue to share with me books on socialism.

Marxism and Adolescence

During 1975, when schools were more often closed than they were open, I channeled my energy into reading every socialist book I could put my hands on. The older children were astonished at the rate I was able to finish reading those Marxist books and my ability to provide them with some analysis.

The first book I read was *Dialectical Materialism* by Henri Lefebvre, outlining a philosophical approach to reality derived from the writings of Karl Marx and Friedrich Engels. After that, I read Karl Marx's *Das Kapital* and *The Communist Manifesto* by Engels and Marx.

During one of those first political discussions with youths who were at least fifteen years older than me, one thing was for sure: I was unable to connect what I read or thought I understood to the current situation in Ethiopia. Some of the youths were talking about workers' rights. At that time, 90 percent of Ethiopians worked as and for farmers for meager wages. Some of the members of my book club talked about how the military staff were underpaid, as well. I simply didn't have much knowledge or the awareness of these labor issues … but I was overpowered by these elite intellectuals I was hanging around with. I wasn't even a member of the party they were affiliated with. Rather, I was just a trusting but curious, nerdy, book-club kid posing no harm to anyone. In short, I got sucked in.

Even though I later realized they were the members of the secretive EPRP party while I was not, they didn't break the pattern of sharing books with me. The only change I saw was that I was getting more and more left-leaning books on topics such as the Cuban Revolution, China, Russia, etc.

Before 1975 was out, I had probably read over thirty books. I was reading these books in the same way I read school textbooks and the holy books, remembering facts and other information, but I was not in the position to relate these books to the revolution taking place in the country. I also noticed these revolutionary youth were frequently asking me to share my understanding of the books and my views. They were surprised to realize how I was able to relay to them what I read and remembered.

Over time, I grew to like and appreciate the characters I found in the books. I particularly developed a strong appreciation for Che Guevara. Perhaps second to Che, the other person I was fascinated by was Leon Trotsky. I didn't really have much respect for Joseph Stalin, though, due to his brutal approach and how many people he killed. I was influenced by Trotsky because of the finesse in his writing and his intellectual approach to offering solutions, but I felt Stalin to be less intellectual and also similar to the Ethiopian military government. The latter seemed to take a more black-and-white and heavy-handed approach; brutality seemed to be their only or main tactic.

My distasteful feelings toward Stalin and contrary appreciation for Trotsky were born out of Victor Serge's works. Serge was a Belgium-born Marxist poet and historian who joined the Bolsheviks in 1919 after he moved to Russia. His widely-translated works described the conflict of that era. Perhaps Serge, in his vision and writings, was the most influential person on me, sparking my insight on how I saw the inner mechanics of mass revolutions and contradictions. Until I began reading his works, I didn't know a political party could have members with contradictory opinions and values, as was the case with Trotsky and Lenin. As for the mechanics of a political party, I had thought that Lenin did everything himself, but I began to learn that parties had speechwriters, debaters, and people performing other roles in order to promote the parties' agenda.

Toward the end of 1975, the revolutionary youth of my book club started to hand me copies of the propaganda (newsletters, brochures, short booklets, etc.) that was being distributed by the EPRP. One of the papers I read was calling for an end to military rule, the unrestricted respect of democratic rights, the formation of a representative government, and the cessation of the repression of dissents. It was after I started reading this literature that I finally started to connect some of the dots, but I still was not clear on the magnitude of what was happening in my own country and the impacts of the movements or the literature being written and distributed.

The Red Terror

One afternoon, a couple of guys from the book club and their siblings asked me to take part in a civil demonstration against the ruling military government. I naïvely agreed to join them.

A bunch of us walked at least seven kilometers (4.3 miles) to the starting point of the demonstration. I had never been to that part of the city and was concerned about how I would find my way back home in case I became separated from my friends. My friends gave me a pile of revolutionary pamphlets to hand out to the people who were standing by in the streets and shops.

I was also directed to pass the pamphlets on to drivers and passengers on the street we were on. This went for about forty minutes or so before I heard a single gunshot. Suddenly, everyone around me started to run for their lives. The gunshots continued and ditto for deafening screams. I ran. I had no clue which direction I was going. I kept running, and after about forty minutes, I was tired and took refuge at an old house. (I guess maybe this was my first marathon training session!) I had been hiding in the abandoned house for about twenty minutes when I was captured by soldiers in full military garb. They beat me with their sticks and tossed me onto the back of a truck.

While I was piled up on the truck with a bunch of revolutionary students who were all several years older than I was, a girl was sitting on my head. I asked if she would move a bit so that I could lift my head from the truck bed and breath properly. As she adjusted her position, she noticed blood was covering my head and face.

She immediately started screaming, "My God! It is my period!"

I had no clue what she was talking about, as no one had ever spoken to me about women's monthly cycles.

I was perplexed about the correlation of her sitting on me and the blood on my face and head. I didn't feel any pain, but when I placed my hand over my head, I felt a lump and a cut on my skull. When I pulled my hand away from my head, I saw it was full of blood. I was shocked as I didn't remember being hit.

The girl then saw the cut on my head and shouted out, "Oh my gosh. They cracked your head open!"

She was more frightened than I was. She quickly took off her sweater and wrapped it around my head to stop the bleeding.

We were a group of around fifty students and were driven for about an hour to a remote location somewhere in the country. I had no inkling where we were or which direction we had been taken from the city.

We were asked to jump off the truck, and the officials started to count and take an inventory of us. One of the officers forcefully removed the sweater that was wrapped around my head. By then, the bleeding had already stopped. But I had a huge headache and was feeling dizzy.

Once we were counted and recorded, we were assigned to rooms. I was assigned to room seven in the maximum-security area of the central political jail. Later I found out the jail was called *Maekelawi*.[2] For a couple of days, I didn't know where I was or why I was there. My primary concern when I arrived was that I would not be able to return home before the 6 p.m. curfew my aunt had put on me. I didn't even know how to tell my aunt what I was doing and where I had ended up that evening. Turns out, explaining to my aunt what I had been up to was the least of my worries.

At the jail, my head was shaved excluding the area where the injury was inflicted. I asked politely if the officer could show me the extent of my head injury. He lifted a mirror over my head to show it to me. There was at least a three-centimeter-long (1.2 inches) cut on my head, but thankfully, it was already healing. To this day, I have a scar as a permanent reminder of the time I was first arrested for being a revolutionary, and I still get headaches as a result of the injury.

Room seven was roughly sixteen-square meters (52.5 feet) for about thirty people. Everyone was older than me—eighteen and above: high school graduates, university students, and professional employees. I started to wonder if anyone from my neighborhood had been captured.

Due to my age and diminutive physical status, almost everyone was looking at me strangely; I was fourteen, but I probably looked more like I was around ten.

Detainees were not allowed to leave the room. We slept head to toe, packed in the room like sardines. All the rooms in the facility were the same size, but detainees were arranged in rooms according to the type of political crime they had committed. Some were there for attempting to change the government or organizing labor strikes, others were arrested for actively recruiting members to the opposing political party, and a few had attempted to kill members of the governing party. Still others, like me, were simply demonstrating against the sitting government. The entire time I lived in the US and tried to explain my culture and personal history to Americans, the only thing that most Americans were unable to grasp was why people in other countries get arrested or even killed for holding a different political view.

That is the fundamental understanding of democracy. In Western society, we say "this is democracy": the ability to express your views without being killed. You simply disagree with someone and move on. The social and political contract in the West means if the president of the US and the Prime Minister of Canada or Britain disagree, for example, they sit down and talk. In the end, although they may leave a meeting having "agreed to disagree," they shake hands and carry on instead of leaving a meeting wanting or plotting to kill each other. In the East, however—and it doesn't matter which country you are talking about—the moment you disagree with someone, you become their enemy and, because of the history of tribal and ethnic conflict, killing the enemy is a natural response to ideological disagreements. This is an oversimplified view, but in short, this is the fundamental difference between Western and Eastern mentalities.

What is now happening in the West and in particular the US, though, with increasing numbers of riots and killings because of ideological differences and racial tensions? Is the West moving away from the expectation that people can disagree without viewing one another as the enemy? Considering some high-profile events of recent years, it's not surprising that pundits and even everyday citizens have started to pose this question. *Is* the West becoming more extreme? When looking at both the left and the right, it could be argued that we are facing the potential diminishment of democracy. Is the pendulum swinging from one end to the other?

Time will tell ….

XVII

Glimmer

First you must ask him to what class he belongs, what his social origin is, his education and profession. These are the questions that must determine the fate of the accused. That is the meaning of the Red Terror.

— Martin Latsis

Room seven, where I was detained, was closer to the washrooms and shower facilities than the other rooms, which was the only advantage to our situation. I made every effort to have a seat near the entrance of the room. To be able to sit near the door was a nearly impossible task, as these were desirable spots. When sitting there, one could get some fresh air and see the sky. It was considered prestigious to be able to work or sit in the sunlight. We only saw the sky on the way to washrooms for about two minutes, maximum twice in a day.

Also, anyone sitting near the door could see other detainees who were passing by to use washrooms, and many of us were wanting to see if other friends or neighbors were incarcerated with us. When I had managed to sit there one day, I recognized one of the guys walking by. His named was Berhane. He was in a different room, and I saw him only that one day as he walked to the washroom. On another day, I also saw the girl who had wrapped my head with her sweater to stop the bleeding. She gave me an acknowledging smile, relieved that I was still alive and okay.

In jail, you see a different side of humanity. Yes, the conditions were awful, and we lived in constant fear and uncertainty of our futures. But that fear and instability, the terrible conditions that everyone is forced to endure, also bring people together. Friday evenings were the most terrifying times, as we were instructed to have supper an hour early. Once supper was served, we heard a truck being parked outside the gate while the engine continued idling. The guard called names and dragged out the youths from the individual cells, taking them out to meet the death squads. During the first two Fridays, I was busy digesting what was transpiring, the process that was unfolding, and the impact on fellow detainees. Ironically, I had felt more scared as a child left alone on the street than I was feeling when I was in the political jail. Primarily, I was too young to fully comprehend what was happening in jail, and because I had committed no major political violations, I didn't think I would get killed.

We knew that at dinnertime people would be taken and killed, so we were always on edge, and everyone was supportive of one another, wondering who would be next in line for massacre. In jail, everyone is suffering the same hardships, and everyone is essentially of the same status regardless of their standing in the outside world.

There is a certain comradery and a type of bonding that unfolds in jail that doesn't occur under any other circumstances. Everyone in the room equally shared and rotated the duties of washing the dishes and scrubbing the floor. Other than needing to do those minor housekeeping tasks, we had free time. To keep ourselves occupied and entertained, the detainees arranged and held different activities during the day. In the morning, after the bathroom break, we ate breakfast. Once the breakfast was served, the detainees ran entertainment sessions followed by intense political debates—both philosophical, as well as relating to the current affairs of the country. We kept ourselves busy with storytelling, political discussions, housekeeping, singing, whistling, drama, etc.

The detainees also found ways to create a checkerboard and game pieces. A checkerboard was improvised by drawing on the floor of the cell, and up to thirty pieces each of black and white stackable counters were made for playing. The game pieces were made of toilet paper, light tea, and dark coffee. The detainees formed the pieces by wetting the paper with tea and coffee to make them two different colors (tea for "white" and coffee for "black") and adding sugar when the paper was still wet. Once the paper dried, the sugar made it stay firm.

When I was in Nazreth and playing gebeta, I had thought there should be another game I master. In jail, I carefully watched how checkers was played and paid extra attention to those who managed to consistently win the game. I quickly realized that making the pieces king on the checkerboard was the key to winning. The king can move forward, backward, and diagonally, so it's easier for a king to capture the opponent's game pieces. I noted that if a player continued jumping and capturing their opponent's checkers until they were all removed from the board, he would win!

I started to play the game, and as I got better at capturing the other players' checkers, I came up with ways all my opponent's pieces would be blocked so that my opponent couldn't make any more moves. From having my ass kicked out of the game within five minutes, I quickly started to beat the most skilled players in the room. The same nickname followed me to the detention center: the Chu Che—the kiddo!

Déjà vu! Nothing made me feel better than feeling like I had already experienced something that was, in fact, happening for the first time. I had a lot of experience playing the game of gebeta, and I was usually the winner. Likewise, I quickly caught on to checkers and became one of the best players. These types of events helped me gain a lot of confidence as I grew older, and I quickly began to realize ... knowledge is power!

A few gifted youths danced and sang songs. Because the rooms were small, only three or four people could stand and dance at one time, so they took turns dancing and singing for the rest of us. Some were traditional Ethiopian dances and songs, but most were Western. Nearly all the youth in the room had memorized the lyrics of the Black American Motown songs from the 1960s. Although some of the songs they sang, played, and danced to were recorded long before I was born or before I was old enough to remember, it was a thrill for me to listen to them for the first time.

Among the songs they played in jail were those of The Beatles, James Brown, The Supremes, Bob Dylan, Aretha Franklin, Elvis Presley, and Marvin Gaye. Later in life, I learned the name of the songs. Today, when I compile YouTube® video clips of pictures of my travels, hiking trips, and marathon races, I use some of these songs from jail as a backdrop: "A Change Is Gonna Come," by Sam Cooke; "I'd Rather Go Blind," by Etta James; "Turn Back the Hands of

Time," by Tyrone Davis; "If Loving You Is Wrong," by Luther Ingram, and more. The music helps me reminisce about my childhood days, even though I lived under difficult and frightening circumstances. Often, I lose myself in the mix, recalling those days and pondering my experiences.

Ironically, these entertainment sessions in jail were perhaps the first efficiently organized group activities I had seen up to that point in my life. I enjoyed the entertainment.

Spared

One afternoon as we were walking back to room seven on the way back from our washroom break, the head of the jail yelled, "STOP!"

We all froze because we didn't know what or who he was calling for or why. He pointed his index finger at me and ordered me, "Come here! Come here!"

I approached him and stopped about four feet away from his face. He asked me if I was a prisoner. I said I was.

"How long have you been here?" he asked.

I told him I had been there about four months.

He turned his head to the room where the women were kept and, holding my arms, he asked the ladies if I had been born there or if I had been arrested and brought there. They told him that I was a detainee, as I had stated. He turned back to me and asked me a few more questions. Finally, he lifted my arm to see if I had hair under my armpit. There was none. After I had responded to all his questions, he ordered me to go back to my room immediately.

As I was walking back to my room, I glanced at the ladies' room where the women detainees were kept, room one. One of the women beamed at me with a big smile and gave me the thumbs-up sign. She must have been about twenty-two; she was young, but as a fourteen-year-old boy, I thought of everyone else in the jail as old. I wasn't sure what she meant by smiling at me and giving me thumbs-up.

Upon my reaching room seven, several of the men quickly ushered me inside and started to talk to me. I was confused as to what was happening at that moment. Why was I getting such attention?

The oldest of the detainees looked at my face, and he said, "I have been here for almost eight months. You will be the first human being to be released from this jail." He added, "Chu Che, you will be free!"

"An average of fifty men are taken each week and murdered," he continued. "As more prisoners are arrested and brought here, the jail runs out of space, and so the prisoners who have been here the longest are killed. Good luck, kiddo! You will be the first to be freed."

Some of the detainees' relatives in the outside world didn't know where their loved ones were being detained; they weren't aware of this facility. Some people in the city knew about the jail, but others didn't know it existed, so the disappearance of their loved ones was surely a worry for family members. Nearly half of the university students who came to Addis Ababa to attend university and had been captured were from distant provinces. Some perhaps knew they would be assassinated, so after the jail head had pulled me aside, other detainees began to ask me if I could notify their relatives about them. There was a bit of a celebratory atmosphere directed toward me as everyone knew I was about to be released because of my age.

I was the only person rumored to be released from the jail at that time, and the others bombarded me with information they wanted to relay to the outside world. One of them was a young man—a typical first- or second-year university student around twenty-two. He asked me to find his parents after my release and tell them where he was. The challenge was that I didn't have the means, nor did I know the city well enough to roam around to find and then notify the relatives of these detainees as to what had happened to their missing loved ones. I had been put in an awful position, as I knew the families of these detainees would want to know what happened to their loved ones, but I had no way of passing on the information.

The oldest detainee was correct. A few days after my interaction with the jail head, exactly four months and three days after I had been captured, I was released. The head of the jail, a man who killed fifty people a week, simply let me go.

However, after leaving the jail gate, I had no choice but to return and speak to him.

"I don't know where I am, and I don't know how to get home," I told him. I needed his help.

After asking me the area where my family lived, he gave me fifteen cents as bus fare and instructed me to take bus number six to head home. A brutal murderer can send an underaged child home scot-free, even giving the child bus fare. Life is strange!

Torment

This infamous torture house (Maekelawi) was closed in 2018, and the Human Rights Watch[1] reported that Maekelawi was opened for the first time to the public in September 2019. People can now visit as tourists. I only fully realized the magnitude of this jail and the situation I was in while compiling information for this book.

During my four-month stay, an average of fifty people per week were killed by the jail guards. We could count the number of executions by tracking how many times per day we heard the big metal door clang shut anytime the guards came to pull someone out of their room to be taken and shot. The conditions were terrible; when people were beaten and tortured, many of them developed sores, which then fostered gangrene. Detainees would have their wrists tied at their ankles, forcing them into the same position a pig or goat would be if you roasted it on a spit, and the guards would then flip the detainees over, beating and torturing them. Open sores would then rot before they had a chance to heal. Some people died from the torture, and of those who survived, some still cannot walk upright today. Even now, I have occasional nightmares about my time in Maekelawi. I sometimes wake up in the middle of the night in a panic having envisioned and relived events from this period of my life in my sleep.

Between 1976 and 1977, when I was fourteen and fifteen, I was jailed three times. After my first arrest and subsequent release from Maekelawi, I was arrested a second time in a case of mistaken identity.

One day, the government was looking for the boy who had forged his school certificate for me as he was known as a high-ranking revolutionary; he was also the one who had recruited me for the EPRP. Because I had his name on my certificate and was therefore known by the same name, another neighborhood boy pointed to my aunt's house, and I was arrested. My aunt tried to fight the special agents, but of course they overpowered and threatened her. One of them pulled a gun on her, and they also told her they would blow up her gate if she fought back. She risked her life that day trying to save me from being arrested.

They took me away for several weeks until a man who worked with the actual boy in political movements came to verify the boy's identity. When the man saw me, told the guards, "That's not him. You have the wrong person." Then I was released.

Most of the time, when a person was captured, there was no due process or representation by legal professionals. Often, the guards didn't know who they had captured, nor was there a registry of the captures, and no questions were asked. I was lucky to not be killed for mistaken identity or to be a victim of the random killings.

The final time I was arrested was when the government jailed everyone in the community. It was at a period when I witnessed the beating of one of the community members in front of a group detainees, killing him. My third time being locked up was also for a four-month span. I was held in different jails each time I was arrested.

The more I became engaged with the revolutionary youth activities, the more I witnessed the massacre of people and saw acquaintances languishing in jails or fleeing the country. The military government was getting the upper hand in controlling the EPRP movement, and I started to question everything I stood for. Moreover, I was distressed to learn a couple of good childhood friends who were never part of any student movement had been killed for being mistaken as revolutionaries. One of my friends from the book club, who was never involved with any party, had a minor argument with his stepmother, which prompted her to kick him out of the house one night. A revolution guard found him on the street near his house and arrested him. The boy was jailed with me, and one day, the jail guard beat him to death in front of us. The boy was killed for nothing.

Other friends in the jail were set on fire and tortured in other ways, and subsequently had zero ability to walk to the washroom. Still now, I'm unable to unsee or forget those images. And even now, I often think about the boy who wanted me to tell his parents that he was in Maekelawi. To this day, I regret that I could not do that for him.

Yet, the revolution itself and being arrested became a turning point for me. These events served as the catalyst for my finally moving to North Yemen. Had the revolution never happened and had I never been arrested, I would have had no reason to leave Ethiopia as a teenager. Other kids like me who had parents and other relatives outside of Ethiopia did the same. We left in search of better circumstances.

*

As I was reading and reaching out to various individuals who were jailed at Maekelawi, I learned room one, where the girls were kept, was targeted for regular rapes and beatings. One of the female detainees delivered a baby while she was in detention.

When an open society has little respect for women, the situation for women in a closed political jail means their suffering is twice as harsh as that of their male counterparts.

XVIII

Comrades

I don't care if I fall as long as someone else picks up my gun and keeps on shooting.
— Che Guevara

During winter 2019, as I was outlining for this book the major events that took place in my life, I realized there was no option to skip the scariest chapter of my life: the Ethiopian Revolution, which entailed the detainment and the execution of the Ethiopian future (youth) between 1976 and 1977.

I wasn't born to a revolutionary intellectual family. At the age of fourteen, I wasn't allowed or even old enough to enter a cinema, but I was thrown into a jail with high-ranking political activists the government deemed dangerous. I was out of place and unmatched to the narrative of the time.

When I mention to people that I was in a political jail as a teenager, I see their skeptical looks. My cousin who read the back cover page thought I was making up stories. He simply didn't believe me. He asked why he didn't know about this part of my life for many years.

In addition, during the mid-1980s, when I applied for political asylum in the US, I used the racial prejudices I faced in North Yemen and the political arrests I encountered in Ethiopia as grounds for my application. The Immigration and Naturalization Service (INS) judge rejected my request because he wasn't convinced that I could be old enough to have taken part in the movement let alone have been arrested and detained.

Besides my immediate family, who suffered the impacts of my detainment with me, I found no other person who would be able to assist me in refining and clarifying the gaps for my book around that part of my life.

A distant family member pointed out to me the existence of a person living in Winnipeg, Manitoba, Canada. Ali was the right and the necessary person to consult because he is one of the few individuals who can articulate and describe the situation from the perspective of Ethiopian youth at that time. He wasn't a spectator; rather, he was another young person who was incarcerated multiple times. He was tortured and suffered a great deal during that period. He also lost an older brother and countless close comrades to the hands of the killers.

Ali Hussein Saeed was born in Addis Ababa and is currently residing in Winnipeg. He is the chairperson for the Solidarity Committee for Ethiopian Political Prisoners and Refugees. He is a well-known Ethiopian political poet; he channels his experiences and human rights activism through his poetry. In 2009 he received the Human Rights Commitment Award of Manitoba. He has sponsored over 100 political refugees into Canada, and he and his family work tirelessly to assist asylum seekers. There are several articles about him in the *Winnipeg Free Press* and *CBC Winnipeg*.[1]

I must say, it was a bit of struggle to locate him, as Ethiopians don't use last names, and moreover, most don't even use their real names in their online presence. I recalled my childhood New Testament teaching: "... seek, and you will find ..." (Matthew 7:7). I didn't go to God with my prayers to be answered; rather, I applied my perseverance to the wider literal sense that "effort will be rewarded."

I was eventually able to connect with Ali Hussein Saeed over the phone. I quickly conveyed why I was looking for him and pleaded for his assistance. I shared with him the fact that I vividly recall some aspects of the jail (Maekelawi) that I experienced as an adolescent, but many of my memories were vague. Therefore, I approached the meeting with long list of questions.

For example, what were the room sizes that I was detained in? What was the name of the head of the jail who supervised the executions—the man who gave me fifteen cents upon my release and sent me home via bus number six? What was the frequency and the number of youths who were killed in each round of the massacres? What did the truck idling by the jail gate look like, the one used to transport the revolutionists to kill them? What about the torture chamber and his experience? Since I was young and frail, I wasn't tortured as many were, but I needed information to add the voices of those who were tortured and perished without any record.

I found Ali to be a walking reference book! Here is the depiction of some of our conversations:

"I noticed your Facebook name reads Jawisaw Ali. I also discovered your email is Angaw Abara. What is your real name, if I may ask?"

"My name is Ali Hussein Saeed. Angaw is my late brother's name. I continue to use his name because I don't want him to be forgotten."

"Would you be kind enough to share with me how many brothers and sisters you have and your ranking within the family?" I asked him.

"We were seven children: four boys and three girls. I'm the third child, and Angaw was the second oldest child of the family."

"Can you tell me more about your brother?"

"Well, my brother was a revolutionary and was part of the EPRP movement. He was one of the students who was kicked out of the university because of his political activism on the campus. In fact, before you landed in room seven at the Maekelawi jail, my brother was in the same room. They tortured him, and later on they executed him."

I interrupted him and asked him to tell me about the tortures because I vividly recall some of my fellow inmates were tortured and subsequently unable to walk. In fact, they were crawling and pulling themselves via their butts or needing to be assisted by other inmates to go to the washroom. I needed to know the extent of the beatings.

"Needless to say, the torture was inhumane and brutal. They pulled all of my brother's fingernails out. He also lost his left eye during the beatings." The story left me speechless.

He went on to explain other gruesome details of the torture. I was unable to stomach it. I start to mentally replay the events I witnessed some forty-six years prior. As much as I wanted to hear his story, I was also hoping he would stop talking, because it started to make me sick. I politely listened to him until he ended his description.

Then I asked him how old Angaw was at the time he was detained and executed.

"Twenty-five years old," he said.

When I was fourteen and fifteen, I used to think of those who were twenty-five and who were intellectuals as very old and unreachable. As he was speaking, I realized his brother was only ten years older than I was when I was arrested. The images of those who were taken out of room seven for execution came to my mind.

As he spoke, I was taking notes, and tears started to drop onto the notebook I was writing in. I needed to change the topic, so then I asked Ali how old he was at that time.

"I was twenty-two." Only eight years older than me, but the maturity and intellect level were the distance between Earth and the moon. His age was the average age of the youth I was held with.

I went on to ask about the number of people executed and the frequency. I informed him that in my journal and my book, I had recorded that the executions took place once a week, and between thirty or fifty people were executed each week.

He quickly corrected me and explained the situation as if it had taken place just the day before.

"The truck that used gather the students came on an average three times a week. Yes, it is true, they killed an average of fifty plus students on any given night. However, they collected the students from multiple jails, including Maekelawi. You can say between thirteen and thirty students were executed a week Maekelawi."

I was eager to know more about the infamous truck, and he said, "Don't remind me about the truck, because the UPS trucks you see on the streets of the US and Canada have become a constant reminder of death for me. The shape and color of the UPS trucks are identical to the ones used to transport and kill people and had small, barred windows. Every time I see a UPS truck, I cannot help but think of and imagine that the dead bodies of those students could be in it."

He went on to add, "I was jailed four times, at eleven different jail facilities, for a total of seven years. At one of those jail facilities, we used to wash the trucks and find blood. That is how I knew some were executed while still on the truck."

I quickly jumped into the conversation and asked, "Were they killing the detainees inside the truck?"

"Let me describe to you the situation," he replied. "When they took the prisoners to the remote side of the city for execution, they lined them up in front of a mass grave first. Some students refused to leave the truck, so then they shot them while they were handcuffed inside the truck and dragged them into the ditch. We could see the trucks when they brought them to Kerchele, the central jail. The trucks were washed by the life-sentenced prisoners."

I apologized for not remembering the name of the jail head, which he had told me multiple times, already. Plus, I hadn't taken note of the jail head's rank or role during the killings.

He chuckled, and he said, "Not to worry. His name was Lieutenant Teshome. The commanding officer was named Berhanu. Those two were administering the jails, as well as the execution of the thousands of Ethiopian students from all walks of life. Between 1976 and 1978, the Stalinist military dictator's government in Ethiopia killed as many as 500,000 of the country's citizens in a bloodbath called the Red Terror. The terror grew out of a relatively peaceful movement to end the reign of Emperor Haile Selassie."

I became increasingly interested in how Ali managed to stay alive and when he had landed in Canada. I further asked if he would tell me more about the Canadian Museum for Human Rights, which was established on his behalf in Winnipeg, Manitoba.

His response was brief.

"I came to Canada in 1984. Here are a few video clips on YouTube you could view," and he passed on to me some links.[2]

Finally, he said to me, "As you know, while we were in jail, we never saw the visitors. Mothers brought meals, and the only way a mother learned of the death of her son or daughter was when they returned to her the prisoner's clothing and told her not to come back again." He further said, "There is something you should mention about that jail. There was a girl who committed suicide."

He continued to speak, as if he was reading from a newspaper article stating, "The approximate size of the jail was about 4x4 meters, and the average number per room was fifteen or sixteen people. However, between May 1977 to May 1978, the same room was used for seventy prisoners. People were stuck together from shoulder to shoulder. There was no possible way to lie down. We were suffocating in the room. The ceiling of the room produced condensation, which would drip back down onto us. This resulted in the death of some of the older prisoners who were completely unable to breathe."

"My brother Angaw Hussein and fellow comrades Tessema Dressa and Mesfin Kebede were in the same cell. On May 1, 1975 (May Day), the military dictators killed over 800 people. The jails were exploding with more people."

I went silent. Ethiopians are generous, kind, and good-hearted people. I have no idea where such brutality came to play. It made no sense to me!

"When I think of Maekelawi, I think of a farm. It's a persistent thought. The herding and butchering of people. Another memory I have is the chanting of prisoners. I remember the killers shouting the names of prisoners."

Ali continued, "There are two stories I'd like to share about EPRP prisoners. The first is about a young woman who went by the name of Saba. She was being held at the Derg[3] investigation jail under Captain Takele. She was brutally tortured while being asked to give up the names of her comrades. She refused and endured three to four rounds of torture. Finally, unable to withstand the torture and unwilling to give up names, she found an opportunity in the washroom to commit suicide. During that period, washrooms had large ditches. She wrapped a scarf around herself and drowned herself in the ditch. Hers is a sacrifice that cannot be forgotten."

"The second story," he added, "is about comrade Amde Ashine. He was held both in Maekelawi and Derg investigation jails. He was badly tortured and lost nine out of ten toes. He decided to name his remaining pinky toe as *misikir* which translates to witness. The Canadian Human Rights Museum is a big step for Canada. It was not by any means established for me but, in addition to information about other Red Terror survivors, it features my story under the 'Breaking the Silence' exhibit."

I must say, as much as I was eager to learn more about that era, I was incapable of listening anymore, and so I thanked him and began to end our conversation. I told him that I would be expanding the conversation and creating a section in my book for several reasons: to recognize his continued effort on human rights issues, to add some information about his fallen brother and comrade (Angaw), and to leave a history behind for future generations. I also want to include him in my book as his experience legitimizes my memoir as fact for those who may doubt it.

*

Nikolai Krylenko, commissar for justice of the former USSR is known for saying, "We must execute not only the guilty. Execution of the innocent will impress the masses even more." I shall say that I'm lucky to be alive today after being arrested and detained three different times at three different locations. I was fortunate to have escaped the executioners' bullets. But I also wonder, how many died without any recognition or remembrance?

XIX

Elderly Wisdom

Now that I am sixty, I see why the idea of elder wisdom has passed from currency.

— John Updike

*B*etween 1972 and the end of 1977, I kept in regular contact with Bansser. However, the two four-month stints of my first and third detainment prohibited me from visiting him, and he was concerned about me during those time periods. I was jailed for a total of ten months over two years, between 1976 and 1977, and he had no idea why I had disappeared.

Disappearing for a month or two was fine and didn't cause him to worry because he knew I had to walk a long way to visit him, so I couldn't get there for weeks at a time sometimes. But my disappearing for four months worried him. He eventually knew about the first detainment, as I told him about it before the second and third happened, but I never told him about the second detainment because, in June 1977, when I told Bansser that I had been perusing Marxist-Leninist manuscripts and had participated in a student movement and was arrested, he wasn't impressed, to say the least. The two of us had a lot of debates during this time because, as is typical of any teenager in any culture, I chalked his disagreements with me up to the fact that he was older, so he "didn't understand me."

In one of our disagreements, he put his hand up in front of him, his fingers pointed straight up, and told me, "See how every finger is a different length? This is human society. We are born to not have the same identities."

And then he folded his fingers down so that they all appeared to be the same length and continued to argue, "By cutting off the fingers, communism is trying to make people the same or equal. If we follow communism, we cut off people's individualities and individual opportunities."

He didn't subscribe to communism and felt that my fight was a waste of time.

He also had another powerful bargaining chip. He knew that I always loved to hear stories about my father and was fond of hearing about my father's actions and reactions to many situations. Most importantly, he knew how keen I was to be a son my father would be proud of if he still were alive. Now, as I reflect on my entire life, I recognize that since my father's death, and even up to the present, I have always subconsciously tried to emulate my father and be a man that my father would be proud of.

When I didn't listen to Bansser's advice to stay away from the communist faction, he played his ace.

"Your father used to hang Queen Elizabeth's picture in his living room. He was an imperialist who thought England was his home country even without ever inhabiting it. Unlike many Arabs, he carried a full British citizenship passport. He wouldn't be honored by you or your present deeds," he pointed out. "I'm sure he wouldn't be proud of you."

Gulp. His arrow hit its mark.

He was angry with me because I was putting myself in danger of being killed, and he felt it was a futile fight. The revolutionaries were killing the youth and making a public statement by throwing the bodies next to the food markets, knowing that people coming for their daily produce would certainly see the bodies. They were also targeting the families of those they killed; if it took two bullets to kill a boy, they would go to the mother to demand that the mother pay them to cover the cost of the two bullets they used to kill her son. Parents were not allowed to cry or mourn, and they weren't allowed to take back their sons' bodies for proper burial.

For the first time, my loyalty was split between an admiration for a father I barely remembered yet desperately wanted to honor and the youth I had spent time in jail with, including those who had been executed.

Disagreements with Bansser over this issue because of our ages and the different opinions we held ended after my third detainment, when I saw the friend who was falsely arrested subsequently get beaten and killed simply because of his fight with his stepmom. The sight of that senseless killing and the guilt over knowing how my father would feel about my actions woke me up.

That could be me, I acknowledged when I thought of the boy who had been killed because of his argument with his stepmother. After seeing what was happening to my peers because of the revolution, and after developing a strong relationship with Bansser and learning more about my father, I realized I needed to change my life, and to make a change, I would have to leave Ethiopia. This realization was the tipping point, as I acknowledged how tragic it was that my friend, a nerdy book-club boy who never knew anything except what he had learned in school, had been killed for nothing. I could easily suffer the same fate. And Bansser, one of my biggest supporters and the closest I had ever had to a father figure since my own father had died, was angry with me because I was putting myself in mortal danger. He was the bridge between me and my father's side of my family. I felt it was time to cross that bridge. Being arrested was a wake-up call, opening my eyes to the fact that I had the opportunity for a different life, one that was potentially much better, if I went in search of my paternal roots.

Earlier in my childhood, I had studied the Qur'an and the Jewish Bible as if they were textbooks, not as religious doctrines that dictated how I should live my life. And I approached Marxism the same way. The socialist literature I had been reading in book club and on my own was just that: literature for my own interest. I was willing to die for my beliefs at that time, but I also didn't fully realize what exactly those beliefs were and what I stood for.

What I didn't understand until my adult years was that being arrested saved my life. I was too young at the time to fully comprehend the political climate and the impact that the upheaval was having on society. I wasn't cognitively developed enough to connect all of the dots politically and socially; I was simply following a cause that was important to my friends, so it was important to me. I also earned and enjoyed the bragging rights for being held with high-profile revolutionary youth. It was like being in jail with Charles Manson—not admirable in itself, but I felt a bit like a celebrity by proxy.

A Fresh Start

Bansser suggested I leave Ethiopia. He didn't want me to go to South Yemen, as it was another communist country during this period. His rationale was, why take the trouble to go from one communist country to another? If that was the case, he said I should just stay where I was. His suggestion was that I go to North Yemen or possibly Saudi Arabia as interim stopping points with my ultimate destination as England or the US.

"Your father would be happy to see you getting a Western education. Your father never appreciated the Arab hypocrisy and social rules. What do you think?" he proposed.

After a lot of thought, I agreed with Bansser's suggestion to leave Ethiopia. In September 1976, I had completed grade eight, achieving 98 percent on my provisional exam. Most were surprised with the mark I earned as I had spent a good portion of my teenage years in jail and/or reading up on communism.

I had to share with Emebet and Mamecha my decision to leave Ethiopia. I took a couple of days to gather my thoughts on how to break to news to them. My relationship with my aunt and her husband had morphed to a more respectful relationship if not one based on love. My aunt's husband grew to appreciate me and viewed me as his son. In particular, he consistently praised me in public about my academic abilities.

Mamecha was a man of a few words. Always observant. When he said something, it was always measured and to the point. Unlike my mother's brother, Mamecha was most thoughtful in his actions. He didn't know me at first. I was merely the son of his sister-in-law, born from a father who wasn't even Ethiopian. However, he demonstrated the symbol of a true and generous Ethiopian and over time, our relationship evolved; we developed a strong bond. Whenever he purchased anything for his oldest son, he bought an identical item for me, too. He treated me like an adult, and I grew to have the utmost respect for him. I viewed him as my protector. In fact, I was more worried about his feelings about my plans to head to North Yemen than my aunt's; because of the relationship he and I had developed, I feared I would be hurting his feelings.

After lunch on the day I decided I needed to tell them about my plans, I asked if I could speak to both in private. They both went quiet. Even though it was customary to ask the parents to walk first to a room or a gate, they both stood waiting, knowing nothing about what I would say. They had been through some difficult times with me, including my risky political activities. I saw their hesitation. I walked into the living room and sat in the chair. Moments later, they followed me and sat on the larger couch, side by side.

I leaned forward and said, "I have been in communication with Ahmed Bansser. Despite all the difficulties I have put you through, you haven't given up on me. You're my parents filling the absence left by my mother and father. First and foremost, my apologies for all my shortcomings. And thank you very much for all you have done for me. It didn't come clear to me up until recently all of the effort you put in to help me."

Both listened to me without uttering a word. Waiting to hear what my point was.

I continue to ramble, repeating versions of the same message.

"So, what is that you're trying to tell us?" my aunt asked in her normal, serious manner. "You are talking about Bansser, your father's friend and countryman?"

I acknowledged that she was correct.

"How did you find him?"

"I accidently ran into his dry-cleaning facility when I was in grade four," I said.

"So, you have known him for all these years," she asked me to confirm.

"Yes."

"How did you manage to keep it a secret from us the entire time, and why you didn't tell me?" she asked.

I told her, "I was afraid you wouldn't approve and you would ban me from visiting him."

"I wouldn't do that. Why would I? He is a good person and did his best to assist your mother shortly after your father's death," she added.

That made me feel better, as she seemed to have a positive view of Bansser. She went on to talk more about how good Bansser was. After she finished, she paused, and I finally broke the news.

"I'm thinking of leaving Ethiopia to be with my father's side of the family in South Yemen."

They looked at each other. Then there was a long, deafening pause.

Finally, my aunt spoke.

"I didn't deliver you from my womb, but you're my son. I raised you like I raised my own sons. You're not the only person who suffered from your imprisonment. We did too, as we were worried about you and afraid you would be killed."

"I know, and I'm aware of the trauma I caused. But I must leave this country," I said.

"I'm aware that the current situation in our country is frightening, but to see you leaving us is hard for me to accept," she protested.

I sensed that as much as they wanted me to leave Ethiopia to escape the death squad's bullets, they also weren't ready to let go of the boy they raised as their own.

"We know that you have a brother and sisters from your father's side. Do they know you're heading their way? Have you communicated with them directly?" she asked.

"No direct communication has been established yet. I'm not even going where my family resides," I replied.

My aunt jumped quickly on my revelation, "Where are you going, then?" she asked with a great deal of concern.

"I'm going to North Yemen first. My family members live in South Yemen, Saudi Arabia, and the United Arab Emirates. I can only carry a South Yemen passport right now, and none of these countries issues visas or allows anyone to enter their country with the communist South Yemen passport," I explained.

The room went dead silent again.

She spoke again, beginning to show her frustration.

"Where were the Arabs when you were left on the street in Nazreth? I was the one who found you and rescued you. How dare you to think of leaving us! If you had just paid attention to your schooling and stayed away from this stupid youth movement, you would have avoided jail and the torture that came with it. Why? Why has such a thought crossed your mind to leave us and the country?"

Her husband finally spoke adding, "You're no longer a nephew to my wife or a stranger to me. You're like my son, and you have become a good boy. A good example to my children. So, why do you have to leave?"

I explained to them, "Bansser wasn't aware of my whereabouts during the time I was in Nazreth. My mother and my uncle had negotiated a deal after my father's death that my uncle would assume the responsibility of raising me and salvage whatever assets he could recover from my father's estate. He lost all the money and the farmland that had belonged to my father. My uncle was ashamed of his deed and vanished from the face of the earth without notifying anyone that I was without help. Bansser, who was remotely connected to me, didn't know about my predicament during those two years, but you didn't even know, either. That said, I really appreciate that you came to rescue me ...."

Before I finished, my aunt interrupted, and again asked, "How did you even manage to find Bansser?"

For the first time, I sensed how deeply my aunt and her husband cared about me. Even though they were disappointed that I was choosing to leave Ethiopia for North Yemen, they didn't want me to go because they cared.

I repeated that I had been in contact with Bansser for the past five years in secret. Not only that, I was also frequently visiting a few other Yemeni-Hadhrami individuals—Bagarsh, Baobaid, Ben-Salem, and Baharon. I noticed my aunt's looks of resentment and sadness. Those individuals had all known my father, and I didn't get the chance to know my father in the way they had. They were the collective key to my discovering a large part of my identity that was always missing. I guess she didn't understand that.

"Your father was a British citizen. Why don't you obtain a British passport and travel to England," she suggested.

"That was my hope too, but Bansser advised me that getting a British passport might take longer and be more complicated. He thought it best I travel to North Yemen, change my passport from a North to South Yemen one, and connect with my half brother in Saudi Arabia."

"There is also one other thing. I have to revert my name back to my original name," I said.

That was the moment Mamecha spoke again.

He said, "That is okay if you go back to your original name. What is the possibility of not going public about it, though? As you know, we are a Christian family. In this community, everyone knows you. Is there a way you could just leave the country without getting into the details? It's hard for us to explain that you're not our child and you're actually half Arab with a different identity."

"It's impossible to do that," I said. "First, reverting my name requires publication in major newspapers, and it's a given most people will read about it." I went on saying, "Yes, I'm half Arab, and my name is Adel. Everyone should know that. For most of my childhood, I was ashamed and embarrassed about my identity. I'm not prepared to continue hiding my true identity from anyone. The world must know that. I'm no longer ashamed about it," I asserted. But I also felt guilty that I was pushing back against my family who had rescued me.

I saw in Mamecha's face that not only was he losing a boy he raised but also losing control of an unleashed and independent teenager. He was a man of few words—calm, composed. He gathered himself to clarify his final point.

"It's okay. This is your choice, and we support you. I have come to terms with the fact that you have other family—your father's family. And it will be good for you to connect with your roots. So yes, whatever you choose, we will support you."

I assured him that I would take care of myself.

"We love you and care about you," said my aunt.

I stood up, thanked both of them, and left the room.

There's Still One Mystery

During the six years that I lived with my aunt, her sister— my biological mother—never came to visit me, not once. My mother had other children by then, and my aunt also had seven children. My mother never brought her children to my aunt's house to visit their cousins or me, their half brother.

And my aunt says, even to this day, that she took me in out of love for her sister. My cousin Sahle (my aunt Emebet's fourth child) told me that after I left for North Yemen, my mother started to bring her children to my aunt's house to visit their cousins, but she had kept her distance while I was living with my aunt. Why?

In light of the depth of pain my mother displays when she and I talk about how she gave me up, I can't bring myself to ask her this remaining question, so I can only speculate ....

Was it shame? Perhaps she didn't want to acknowledge that I was her child. But my mother's other children have told me she never forgot me, her firstborn child, and always felt my absence. In that case, I would think she would have been eager to see me grow up.

Guilt? Perhaps, like me, she had buried and suppressed her feelings about having given me up. It's possible she felt so guilty that she couldn't look me in the eye and acknowledge that she had done so. To look in the eyes of her child, who had become homeless and abandoned as a result of circumstances that had forced her to make the choice she did, was quite possibly a pain she couldn't face.

Or maybe at that time and in Ethiopian culture—a man's world—her husband forbade her from making any contact with me. I don't know; only she knows the reason.

Tough Love

Emebet's and Mamecha's love for me was unwavering since the day they took me in. Yes, my aunt Emebet's discipline in the years that I lived with her was harsh, but I was almost impossible to control after having lived on the streets for a couple of years, fighting to support myself. When she found me in Nazreth, I had been living like a wild animal—wandering free, focusing on survival—and she must have often been exasperated by my behavior over the years that I lived with her. In particular, I kept running away, and her only choice in keeping me safe in her home was to restrain me at times.

I distinctly remember how she shrieked when I returned home from my first arrest. After I got off the number six bus, while neighbors were hugging and celebrating that I had returned, my aunt started screaming, as if she'd seen a ghost or a demon. Maybe it was because the poor woman had thought she had finally gotten rid of me and was horrified at the realization that she would have to begin taking care of me again! The wild child had returned!

But in all seriousness, she knew how severe the torture and punishments were in the jail. Unlike other children who were detained, I didn't come out of jail handicapped; others had permanent vision damage, their fingernails had been pulled out, or they had other permanent injuries. I came back relatively unscathed. She was surely shocked, relieved, and grateful that my life had been spared.

She did the best she could to tame me, and I will always be grateful for her support, especially in making sure I continued my education. Even though we weren't allowed visitors in Maekelawi, I felt her presence there with the food she sent. Mamecha and my cousins would bring tea and milk to the jail for me, and after the guards inspected it, I was given my aunt's gifts of food. And that she risked her life for me to the point of having a gun pulled on her and being threatened by the officer who said he would blow her head off if she didn't hand me over the second time I was arrested is testament to her love and concern for her rebellious nephew.

Today, my aunt says it was the EPRP that ruined my world and hers. She remembers me jumping out of the window of her house at night to go and join the EPRP movement's activities.

"In our community, the EPRP was distributing communist and anti-government pamphlets during dawn hours. Some of it was thrown over our fence. From the handwriting, I knew it was his. When I asked him to tell me if he was taking part in the movement, he pretended he didn't understand my question," she remembers.

My aunt was not my birth mother, yet she sacrificed and suffered more for me than any mother ever should over a child. She didn't have to take me in. And once she did, she didn't have to keep me. She could have let me run away and forgotten all about me, but she didn't. When I ran, she looked for me, and when I came back, she chained me up so I would stay safe in her home. My aunt dedicated herself to setting me straight even though she had her own children to raise. Despite all the trouble I caused her, she never gave up on me.

In the process of maturing, I did put through hell those who attempted to control me, particularly my aunt Emebet. I'm not sure if I could ever even have the words to apologize for all the distress I caused her.

It was the love, financial support, and guidance of my aunt, her husband, and Bansser that kept me safe and thriving as I moved through my teenage years and began to figure out who I was. They kept me alive and pointed me toward the path which took me to the next stage of my life.

XX

Exodus

Then Moses stretched out his hand over the sea, and the Lord drove the sea back by a strong east wind all night and made the sea dry land, and the waters were divided. And the people of Israel went into the midst of the sea on dry ground, the waters being a wall to them on their right hand and on their left.

— Exodus 14:21-22

For me to depart the country, I needed a birth certificate and a passport. At the time, passports were not issued for children under the age of sixteen, and I was fifteen. That was problem number one. The next hurdle was that the South Yemen Embassy only issued a travel document that could be used as a one-way travel pass to Aden, South Yemen. If I were to go that route, I would face additional hurdles attempting to leave communist South Yemen to try to get to North Yemen or any country other than socialist countries. The plan was to travel directly to North Yemen or Saudi Arabia, but neither of these countries accepted the travel papers I could get. A passport was required, which I wasn't yet eligible for.

I was also under the impression that I could get a British passport. My father had carried a British passport, and so I was registered in the British Embassy. However, the Tahir family, who had taken over my father's house, had kept all the records and they had refused to surrender the papers. Bansser told me I had a better chance of getting a South Yemeni passport more quickly than a British passport, as the process to get a British passport was much more complicated. Moreover, because all my father's documents were destroyed or hidden, I had no proof of my father's connection to the UK, so my chance of getting a British passport vanished.

I had to wait until September 1977 to approach the South Yemen Embassy, as my birthday is on January 6 and in 1978, when I was turning sixteen, I would be able to obtain a passport.

To get the process started, Bagarsh called me to his office to give me cash and asked me if I had an Ethiopian ID. I told him I did, and he said, "We need it."

I told him, "My ID is useless, as the name on the document doesn't say 'Adel.'"

He didn't read Amharic, so I read my ID to him.

He got angry at me and asked, "Where and how did you come up with such a name?"

I told him, "I needed to register in school, and I used one of my neighbor's children's certificates to get enrolled."

He phoned Bansser and told him, "We are screwed! This fool has an Ethiopian ID with an Ethiopian name!"

He yelled at me, and he kicked me out of his office, telling me to go and sort things out with Bansser before we could proceed. Bagarsh was an overpowering individual. He was loud and demanding. He reminded me of what I imagined my father was like. But despite his overbearing temperament and the differences he had had with my father, he was always kind to me.

Bansser's laundry facility was about one kilometer (0.6 miles) from Bagarsh's office. I walked to Zenith to ask Bansser for advice on how to proceed. He put his two arms behind his back and asked me to follow him.

We walked together for a few blocks, and he informed me, "We must file an application with the court and have your name changed back to Adel."

The judge ordered an ad be put in the local paper and distributed to all police stations in case I had a criminal record or there was opposition to my application. Then he would pass his judgment. Bansser paid the necessary amount for the name change—about fifty Ethiopian birr or the equivalent of twenty-five dollars—and he also arranged and paid to publish an ad in two major national newspapers. Bansser and Bagarsh then made a trip to a couple of courthouses, swearing on the Qur'an that I was Majid's son, and my name was Adel.

In Ethiopia, during those days, there were two types of crimes: the first was crime as we know it in the Western world, such as murder, theft, tax evasion, etc. The second was to be wanted for political activities. It was common at that time for a person to be killed, tortured, or imprisoned for having a different political opinion.[1]

In my case, the judge wanted to check if I was on a wanted list for political activities. Since I had already been arrested, detained, and released, I was considered clear. (When I was released from jail, I signed a paper agreeing to not engage in any further anti-government or public interest activities and was given a certificate confirming I was in the clear.)

The two men and I waited for two weeks and then went back to the court. The court officially changed my name back to Adel, and Bansser and I went on to get a duplicate of my birth certificate from the municipal office. I also had to change my name on my grade six, eight, and ten school certificates so that I could use them in North Yemen to finish school. (Because the schools had been closed so often during the revolution, and the schools therefore didn't have enough room to accommodate all of the students coming through, students had to complete two grades in the same amount of time they previously did one grade. Therefore, I did grades nine and ten in one year—1977—instead of two. Certificates were issued for the provisional exams that students wrote at the end of grades six, eight, ten, etc.)

A month after we had completed all of these steps, we went to the South Yemen Embassy to get a passport. They needed three Hadhramis who had known my father to testify and sign the necessary documents. Baobaid filled out the necessary forms, and Bansser and Bagarsh signed the papers.

The South Yemen consul looked at my face and said, "He doesn't look Yemeni. Are you sure he is Yemeni?"

Bagarsh yelled at him, "What do you mean? His father was as green as I am.[2] He is Hadhrami. I knew his father, and he is his father's son. His name is Adel Majid. As you know, most Hadhramis are dark-skinned. Shame on you for asking this kind of question!"

He concluded, demanding, "Please approve the paperwork and give him the passport so that we can send him to North Yemen."

The room went quiet. Then the consul apologized.

On January 6, 1978, my sixteenth birthday, I picked up my passport. Those three individuals had contributed money toward purchasing my flight ticket and buying me new sets of clothing, and they gave me pocket money I could use when I arrived in North Yemen. And then, each of them gave me advice: Be strong, stay out of trouble, complete your education, don't be a disgrace to your family, good luck, and God be with you!

*

My specific memories and thoughts of those days when I was preparing to leave Ethiopia are mixed. I was filled with a lot of confusion. I was faced with leaving my birthplace and searching for ancestral roots in a different country. I felt I was betraying Ethiopia, the only home I knew at that time. I felt defeated for choosing to depart Ethiopia, where I was still influenced by the revolutionary ideologies and youths. Yet I was also optimistic and excited about starting a new chapter in my life—leaving behind my tumultuous past in Ethiopia and embarking on a new era. Perhaps I was destined to be a Yemeni, and North Yemen was meant to be my transitional home. After all, I am Yemeni. A good portion of my family reside in the Middle East.

I should be there, and I belong there.

*

On Friday, January 13, 1978, I left Ethiopia, becoming one of the droves fleeing the country for better circumstances. Hope in the sky! According to Ethiopian Airlines, the temperature that day was fifteen degrees Celsius (fifty-nine degrees Fahrenheit).

The takeoff time was around 11:30 a.m. My aunt's husband was the one who drove me to the Bole International Airport. My biggest supporter, Ahmed Bansser, was there, too. He must have noticed how nervous I was, and he told me to relax.

"It is only about 1,000 km and a couple hours' flight," he assured me.

His precise information on the distance and duration gave me some comfort, but I was still nervous.

Bansser went on to introduce me to a family who was departing to North Yemen on the same flight and politely asked them to assist me beyond the visitor's area inside the airport. He handed me a bunch of letters and requested that I hand deliver them to another Hadhrami man, my father's friend Ahmed Bawazier, who would meet me at the airport in Sana'a, North Yemen. I tucked the letters into my carry-on bag.

He said the last words he ever spoke to me: "I would love to see you again with a master's degree from London or America! You're smart and competent, and most importantly you're Hadhrami. You can do it!"

I had no clue what a master's degree was supposed to look like or where it came in the order of education. I simply nodded as a form of an "okay, sir" gesture. I hugged him and proceeded through the security check.

Bansser didn't live long enough to see me make it to the US and Canada, so he wasn't able to congratulate me for my achievement when I earned my master's degree. In Calgary, Canada, in 2006, I signed the back of my MBA transcript saying, "Dedicated to Ahmed Bansser!"

*

As I settled into my seat that day in 1978, the plane took off. Watching the city disappear out of the plane window was my last recollection of Addis Ababa.

Preview of Volume Two

Hope in the Sky, the second volume of Adel Ben-Harhara's three-volume memoir, speaks about millions of Yemen's Muwalladin (foreign-born Yemenis) struggling for equal rights and citizenship. He was one young man who spent a dozen years in North Yemen, where he suffered from prejudice, discrimination, and the effects of civil war. He endured harsh treatment because he wore a dark skin, was born in East Africa, and was unable to assimilate into an underdeveloped society living according to primitive cultural traditions. He stood strong and managed to depart his ancestors' land, not because he was tough, but because he had no choice.

What happened to one of the oldest nations on Earth, the cradle of Arab civilization, the home of the biblical Queen of Sheba, consort of King Solomon? Yemen, with ties to the Semitic lands to its north and to the cultures of the Horn of Africa across the Red Sea, is frozen in time and still practicing medieval traditions. Illiteracy and constant tribal conflicts serve as catalysts in suppressing development and modernization and in keeping the country and surrounding areas suspicious and threatening to the world.

Want to learn the inner workings of Yemeni life through the struggles of a sixteen-year-old boy who immigrated to his ancestors' land? Read on.

Preview of Volume Three

The contrast between how the West views newcomers versus how immigrants picture themselves is stark. New residents in Canada and the US are often misunderstood, disrespected, or poorly labeled due to inaccurate assumptions and stereotypes held by all parties.

What does it take to attend university in a second or third language? What are the common denominators amongst people arriving in the West wanting to pursue "the American dream"? What are the impacts of cultural and social adjustments, academic and professional advancement? How do new Canadians and Americans maneuver through prejudices and discrimination coming from not only those born on Western soil but also from other immigrants?

My Silver Lining, the final volume of Adel Ben-Harhara's three-volume memoir, is a window into the hurdles that settlers face and the support they get from those who welcome immigrants to their new chosen homelands. Peer through this window by reading the story of a young man who navigated from Ethiopia and North Yemen to the US and Canada to establish his identity and purpose.

The story shows how Adel Ben-Harhara succeeded after leaving behind everything he knew and attempted to embrace an unknown way of life on a new continent.

Acknowledgments

To be told "you are the son of a woman" is an insult in Ethiopian culture. To become a man, you must be raised by a man. However, having lost my father at a young age, I was then surrounded and raised by women, and I am proud of the man I have become because of these women. Who I am today is testament to the influence of the many strong and admirable women who have been my mothers, sisters, wives, daughters, and friends for six decades.

To My Mothers

I'm the luckiest human because I am claimed by eight different mothers as their own son! I'm a product of their efforts, courage, guidance, wisdom, and most of all, love. I fondly remember the meals they fed me and the trust they put in me to be a better man. How did this happen? As a child and young adult, I moved around between Ethiopia, North Yemen, and the US. A couple of generous families took me in to provide me with the necessities of life. They come from varying backgrounds—different cultures, religions, and ethnicities—but the value they brought to my life is transcending. Today, I pound my chest saying, "Victory is claimed by all, failure to one alone." I begin with my eternal thanks to these women:

Weinishet Fertewehal You, my biological mother, did the best you could with the tools you were given. You gave me life and set me on the path to having all these surrogate mothers who influenced my life in such positive ways. For those things, I am very grateful to you.

I love you because of everything you ever did for me. I love you because you gave me life and gave me the best life you knew how to give. I love you because what has harmed me has also contained the tiniest of blessings. I love you with every cell of my being, and I know you did the best you could.

Rukia Atufa, my first stepmother, lovely lady, you told me, "You're my first son who I didn't deliver." I lived with you between the ages of two and five. For your love and care during those early years.

Emebet Fertewehal, my aunt, my mother's younger sister. For stepping into my life and rescuing me from the streets of Nazreth, for providing me shelter and education, and for sending me off to North Yemen. For putting up with my adolescent troubles. Most importantly, for installing within me a determination to finish what I start. You took me to Coptic Churches (Orthodox) and asked me to read to you the Old and New Testaments. Your husband, Mamecha, asked me to read the newspaper to the neighbors—a role that gave me self-confidence and purpose.

You kept my childhood journals all these years because you recognized I was an A+ student and because you said my handwriting was beautiful. These journals are the record of my life, which I used to write this book. You and Mamecha saw me as a good human, and because of you, I try to be one.

Maryam and **Zeinab Afif**, my two stepmothers in Hadhramaut, South Yemen, for sharing stories about my father with me and educating me about my Yemeni roots and identity. For your pearls of wisdom. For your dignity, charm, grace, and more. Most of my life principles came from you. You taught me to be patient, polite, persistent, and persuasive.

Ms. Abebech, you gave to me when you had little to give; for allowing me to take shelter at your home and for feeding me when you could when I was living on the streets of Nazreth.

Fatuma M. Ali (Banajah), for being a mother figure for me in North Yemen, for opening your house to me, for the meals you cooked for me. You gave me confidence in myself. I owe my huge personality to you. You advised me to be an honest man and seek knowledge over wealth. You told me, "I wish I had a son like you, but I also feel you are my son, regardless."

Norma Rice, my adopted American mother from Boise, Idaho. In the days when no Black people were living in Boise, you took me to live with your family while I was attending Boise State University. You regularly attended my soccer games and kept saying, "That is my son," repeatedly whenever I scored a goal. For being the first woman ever to recognize me in public as her "son." I still fight back tears when I think of that moment. I'm a mix of major religions. Out of respect for you, I attend The Church of Jesus Christ of Latter-day Saints (LDS) services every now and then.

To My Sisters

Hind, Sheikha, Fawzia, and **Muna Ben-Harhara**, for not giving up on me, your nerdy, skinny, dark-skinned, socially awkward half brother from a Christian mother. You are always proud of me and give me the utmost respect even though I am often short in fulfilling my brotherly duties according our Hadhrami traditions.

To My Father Figure

Ahmed Bansser, for being a father figure as much as anyone could be. I had a father, but I didn't know who he was. You were the bridge between me and him. The father I didn't know came to be my father—the man I respected and by whom I defined myself—because of you teaching me about his life and character. My image of everything my father was came to play in my life because you not only provided financial assistance to me, but you connected me to my family. You closed the psychological and physical gap that I had with my Hadhrami family. And you could legitimize me as a complete human. You told me, "You have a father who had character. You have a father who was strong. Your father was principled."

Your daughter, Fawzia, said, "My father didn't do anything special for Adel," and from her perspective, perhaps you did nothing out of the ordinary. However, a good portion of my personality formed because of you. You taught me how to conduct myself. You told me, "Be a man. Think this way." I don't think you knew the consequences of your influence on my life. If you hadn't been there to teach me, I would have turned out to be a completely different person. You were a generous, good person. Beyond that, you created my character.

To My Daughters

Lina and **Summer**, you have brought a positive light into my life. My years, from the age of five, were always rocky. When I reflect on my life, I have a hard time remembering anything good about it, and I was never optimistic about "tomorrow" because of my experiences as a child. You give me a reason to endure and to carry on. You have opportunities I didn't have—you have the chance to experience the positive things that didn't happen to me, the things that didn't occur in my life, and I look forward to seeing you continue to blossom. You give me a reason to live, to hope, to be optimistic. You don't have to bring anything to the table; you don't have to do anything. Your presence—just the fact that you exist—gives me a reason to look forward.

To My Contributors

Al-Hamadi, Bazaraa, Al-Habshi, Baobaid, Bawazir, Ali Saeed, Bahmam, Sahle Mandefro, and *Janine Shum.*

ساهلي مانفريدو ,باهمام ,علي سعيد ,باوزير,باعبيد ,الحبشي ,بازرعة ,الحمادي,
جنين شوم

Thank you!

For complete information on the team members who worked on my books, visit adelbenharhara.com/team.

From Lorna (Co-Author)

When Adel first approached me about working with him, I immediately knew this was a project I wanted to be involved in.

"I need a ghostwriter to assist me with my memoir. I have an outline and am gathering old journals, historical records, and related materials. It's my father's story and mine combined, covering three continents as well as a few religions, languages, cultures, and everything in between," was what his initial message read.

Adel and I officially began working together a few weeks after he sent me his first draft; once I started to read through it, I was glad he had tackled the first draft himself. What he was able to rough out in a few weeks would have taken me several months, and I daresay I would have not been able to capture his voice as well as he presented himself. It was a win-win: I had a plethora of rich material to work with, and my invoices were going to be a lot smaller than they would have been had I started the writing from scratch!

I'm not the ghostwriter of this book. Adel did the majority of the writing; I did some. I added a paragraph here, a sentence there. Much of my role was more of a coach and structural and stylistic editor. My focus was on guiding him through reordering the content, rephrasing chunks of it, and prompting him to dig more deeply into his memories to fill in gaps and fill out stories.

Like Adel, I'm not a fan of applying one specific label to people, but for ease, we chose "co-author" to attach a name to my role, which included writer, editor, sounding board, and both teacher and student. And we both provided a great deal of comic relief to the other. What started out as a respectful, easy-flowing professional relationship ended up feeling like more of a brother-sister relationship, with us teasing and pranking each other on phone or Zoom calls or by leaving silly notes in the manuscript now and then for the other to find and laugh over. He quickly realized that anything he told me in conversation or anything he sent me via text message was potential content for the book (pending his approval, of course)! Despite my teasing him at times that "I might put that in the book, you know," he was never hesitant about being completely open, honest, and vulnerable with me.

Helping someone write their life story requires a lot of trust on both sides, and we had endless in-depth conversations about what should be included and why. As Adel revealed his life story to me, he included details of his life that he thought are too personal or simply irrelevant for the books. I'm humbled and honored that he trusts me with the details of his life.

Through my conversations with Adel, I quickly realized that I was working with a man who is intelligent, resilient, resourceful, and also damn funny. Although he is small, Adel is a force, and he has a voice that is bigger than his body. After reading his first draft, I learned that he had fought his way to the clichéd better life, and when I met him in person, I saw that he seemingly has a permanent smile on his face. He *is* always smiling, if not with his mouth, at least with his eyes. I've made enough trips around the sun, though, to have learned that many of us who project a constant, boisterous, positive outlook are also often hiding deep scars behind our smiles, and Adel certainly fits into this category.

In my days as an ESL teacher working with people from all over the world (Afghanistan, Iran, Iraq, Libya, Sudan, Russia, China, South Korea, Thailand, Mexico, etc.) who had come to Canada to seek a better and often safer life than the one they were leaving behind, I was humbled every day by their personal stories. My struggles are real, but they are, as we in Canada have flippantly said for years now, "first-world problems." Someone cut me off as I was driving down the highway; my next-door neighbors play their music too loudly; someone lets their dog do its business on my lawn and doesn't pick it up; it's been -30 degrees for a whole week now—poor me in my 1,600 square foot house with central heating.

No one's life is always easy. But we all view our lives through whatever lenses we choose to place in front of our eyes. Even in the most difficult circumstances, there may be those who throw in the proverbial towel and become discouraged or downtrodden, or even perish. But there are others who, regardless of what may be on their plate figuratively and literally, make the decision to swallow what they've been dished, stick a smile on their face, and forge ahead with an open mind, a welcoming spirit, and an ebullience that is admirable and infectious. And they actively look for better options to place on their plates.

Adel is unequivocally the latter. His smile, humor, and zest for life are contagious, and intelligent thought spills out of him with every word he expresses. At the age of five, he could have given up and had he done so, his life would have taken such a drastically different turn than it did. Yet his desire then and now to learn, read, and exercise his brain and his body have contributed to him becoming a teeny man who has lived and continues to live an oversized life, not merely taking opportunities that come his way but creating opportunities and making his life happen. He doesn't just live his life; he has built one, and in doing so, has impacted and inspired many along the way, including me. I know his story will inspire you, as well.

— Lorna Stuber

Website: lornastuber.com
Facebook: facebook.com/lornastubereditor

Glossary

Except as noted, the terms in this glossary are nouns. Those that refer to a specific person or place are capitalized. Those that refer to a generic item are not capitalized. Any terms that are not nouns are noted with information in brackets after the term. Where applicable, the language of origin of the term is included before the definition. Additional spellings are included with a /.

Ababe - አበበ
(Amharic) one of Adel's half brothers on his mother' side.

Abebayehosh - አበባየሆሽ
(Amharic) During Enkutatash (Ethiopian New Year), a traditional song called "Abebayehosh" is performed by groups of Ethiopian girls who approach families in their neighborhood to extend best wishes for the New Year. In return for their singing, the girls receive blessings from the elders.

Abebe Bikila - አበበ ቢቂላ
(Amharic) Abebe Bikila (August 7, 1932-October 25, 1973) was the first Ethiopian and African Olympic gold medalist and won his first gold medal while running barefoot in the 1960 Summer Olympics in Rome. Bikila won back-to-back Olympic marathons in 1960 and 1964. He ran both marathons in world-record time.

Abebech/Ms. Abebech - ወይዘሮ አበበች
(Amharic) the lady who provided shelter for Adel between 1970 and 1972 while he was left homeless in Nazreth.

Abubaker Bagarsh -ابوبكر باجريش
(Arabic) the son of Salem Bagarsh and classmate of Adel's brother, Hussein.

Addis Ababa - አዲስ አበባ
(Amharic) the capital and largest city of Ethiopia; means "new flower"; known in Oromo as Finfinne, "natural spring."

Ād/Ādd/Āde - عاد

(Arabic) one of the ancient Arab tribes (the "lost Arabs") located in Southern Arabia. The people of this tribe (the Ādites) were regarded as one of the original groups of Arabs who rejected the teachings of a monotheistic prophet named Hud. They formed a prosperous nation until they were destroyed in a violent storm; the storm is mentioned several times in the Qur'an in verses 41:16, 46:24, 51:41, 54:19, and 69:6.[1]

Agaw/Agew/Agäw - አገው
(Geʿez/Amharic) a Cushitic ethnic tribe inhabiting Ethiopia and Eritrea, historically noted by travelers and outside observers to have practiced what some described as a "Hebraic religion," although some practiced Ethiopian Orthodoxy, and many were Beta Israel Jews.[2]

Ahmed Bansser/Bansser - أحمد بانصير
(Arabic) Adel's father's close friend and countryman from Hadhramaut; a father figure who played a significant role in Adel's young life and was instrumental in connecting Adel with his relatives in South Yemen.

Aksum/Kingdom of Aksum
The ancient Kingdom of Aksum was in power from the second to the tenth century and covered what is now northern

Ethiopia as well as modern-day Eritrea, eastern Sudan, and Yemen. Its capital was the city of Aksum (Axum).

Alemayehu Belayneh - አለማየሁ በላይነህ
(Amharic) the boy who assisted Adel in forging the school certificate. He was a revolutionary and social activist and a childhood role model to Adel.

Aramaic
(Amharic) a Semitic language that originated in the ancient region of Syria.

areki - አረቄ
(Amharic) a colorless, clear traditional alcoholic beverage most often distilled in homes.

Asr - صلاة العصر
(Arabic) afternoon prayer. Asr is one of the five mandatory Islamic prayers. Because an Islamic day starts at sunset, the Asr prayer is the fifth prayer of the day. It is the third prayer of the day when counting from midnight.

Awadh Baqehum - عوض باقحوم
(Arabic) former national Ethiopian soccer player who played in the 1960s; his father was a friend of Adel's father.

Aynalem - አይናለም
(Amharic) one of Adel's cousins. One of Emebet's and Mamecha's daughters.

Baharon - باهارون
(Arabic) Haron Baharon was Adel's childhood friend in North Yemen. Salem Baharon, Haron's uncle, was a good friend of Adel's father and lost his life during a cosmetic surgery.

Bahomed - باحميد
(Arabic) the man who was accidently killed by Adel's father during a hunting trip in Ethiopia.

Baobaid - باعبيد
(Arabic) a good friend and classmate of Adel's older brother, Hussein; instrumental in getting Adel a South Yemen passport and sending him to North Yemen.

Basherahil - با شراحيل
(Arabic) Abduallah Basherahil was a friend of Adel's father. Adel's mother worked for the Basherahil family as a nanny prior to giving birth to Adel.

Bekele Mola - በቀለ ሞላ
(Amharic) the man who borrowed money from Adel's father and then offered to pay back only a fraction of the loan after Majid died. He was the first Ethiopian to construct hotels and motels in towns and tourist centers throughout the country. At least thirteen hotel establishments in the Ethiopian Rift Valley region carry his name.

berbere - በርበሬ
(Amharic) a traditional blend of ginger, chiles, cardamom, cinnamon, and nutmeg from Ethiopia and Eretria used to season stews called *wats* (see *doro wat*).

Belaye
(Amharic) the father of Adel's friend Alemayehu.

Chu Che - ቹቸቹቸ
(Amharic) a nickname meaning "kid" or "kiddo."

damoz - ዳሞዝ
(Amharic) one of the three main types of marriage practiced in Ethiopia; the least formal of the three.

Dembiya - ደምቢያ
a historic region of Ethiopia, near the city of Gondar and by Lake Tana, in northern Ethiopia.

Demera - ደመራ
(Amharic) the burning of a bonfire on the eve of the Ethiopian Meskel Festival. On that day, the celebrants light a bundle of sticks and let the smoke fly high in the sky.

Dhuhr/Zuhr - صَلَاة ٱلظُّهْر
(Arabic) noon prayer; one of the five mandatory Islamic prayers. Because an Islamic day starts at sunset, Dhuhr is the fourth prayer of the day. It is the second prayer of the day when counting from midnight.

doro wat - ዶሮ ወጥ
(Amharic) chicken stew; "doro" means chicken, and "wot" means stew.

Eid - العيد
(Arabic) Eid marks the end of Ramadan and is celebrated by decorating and gathering for feasting on special food and drink.

Emebet Fertewehal - እመቤት ፈርተወሃል
(Amharic) Adel's aunt (his mother's younger sister) who took him in after discovering he was abandoned and homeless.

Enkutatash - አዲስ ዓመት
(Amharic) Enkutatash is the New Year public holiday in Ethiopia and Eritrea. It occurs on Meskerem 1 on the Ethiopian calendar, which is September 11 (September 12 during a leap year) on the Gregorian calendar.

Eyou Beliyou/Jubilee Elementary School
(Amharic) the elementary school Adel attended between
1972-1973, which was located adjacent to the Imperial Palace.
The school was built for children of the employees who
worked at the palace. After the fall off the Imperial system in
Ethiopia, the school was closed, and the facility and the
surrounding land were made part of the palace.

Fajr - صلاة الفجر
(Arabic) dawn prayer; one of the five mandatory Islamic
prayers. An Islamic day starts at sunset, and the Fajr prayer is
the third prayer of the day. If counted from midnight, it is the
first prayer of the day.

Falasha - ፈላሻ
(Amharic) a derogatory name meaning "stranger" or "exile"
to refer to Ethiopian Jews, who were prohibited from owning
land or obtaining an education.

Falasha Mura - ፈላሻ ሙራ
(Amharic) the name given to members of the Beta Israel
(Jewish) community in Ethiopia who did not follow Israelite
law or were converted to Christianity, either voluntarily or by
force.

Fasika/Fasica - ፋሲካ
(Ge'ez, Amharic) Easter, also called *Tensae* ("to rise"). The
death and resurrection of Jesus is much more significant than
his birth in Orthodox and Ethiopian Evangelical theology, so
Fasika is more significant than Christmas.

Fawzia - ፋውዚያ - فوزية
(Arabic) one of Adel's half sisters; Bansser's daughter has the
same name.

Ferdows Munir - فردوس منير - ፉርዱስ መኒር
(Arabic) Rukia's niece; she was a role model for Adel.

Galla - ጋላ
(Amharic) an Ethiopian tribe also known as the Oromo;
"galla" means "free men." The Galla are one of the largest
racial groups in Ethiopia.

gebeta/gebata - ገበጠ
(Amharic) generic term for various mancala games played in
Ethiopia and Eritrea.

Genna/Ganna - ገና
(Amharic) Genna (Christmas) in Ethiopia is on January 7. It
is an important Ethiopian holiday, although not as important
as Easter (see *Fasika*). Ganna is twelve days before Timket,
the Ethiopian Orthodox celebration of Epiphany.

Getahun - ጌታሁን
(Amharic) Adel's cousin who became like a brother to Adel
while Adel was living with Getahun's parents, Emebet and
Mamecha.

Ghusl/Gusl - الغسل
(Arabic) "full ablution"; involves the mandatory full-body
purification before performing various rituals and prayers.
Ghusl is required for full purification in any of the following
cases: after sexual intercourse or ejaculation; after
menstruation has finished; if one has touched a dead body;
after irregular bleeding in women; after vaginal discharge
following childbirth. It is also performed on the body of a
dead Muslim.[3]

Gondar
The former capital of the Ethiopian Empire. Gondar has been
called the "Camelot of Africa" as it is home to several royal
castles, including those in the UNESCO World Heritage site
Fasil Ghebbi.[4]

Haj Munir - الحاج منير
(Arabic) a friend of Adel's father, Haj Munir had eleven
children, many of whom Adel played with when he was a
child. Several of them are still alive, and Adel has been in
touch with them as he gathered information for his memoir.
Haj Munir's children were Rukia's nieces and nephews.

Hamle - ሐምሌ
(Amharic) the month of the Ethiopian calendar that coincides
with July 8-August 6 in the Gregorian calendar.

Hammurabi Code
a collection of 282 rules written at the end the reign of
Hammurabi, the sixth king of the Babylonian dynasty. These
laws were carved onto a massive black stone and outlined
regulations for commercial transactions and the fines and
punishments for violating the rules.

Hassan - حسن
(Arabic) a classmate and friend of Adel whom Adel met
during his runaway days in Addis Ababa. Hassan assisted Adel
in finding a place to sleep and learning to shine shoes.

Himyarite/Himyar
The Himyarite Kingdom was the government in the southern
highlands of Yemen from 115 BC-570 AD and was at its
height in 525 AD before being overthrown by Christians from
Ethiopia.

Hind - الهند

(Arabic) Hind, also known as Mujudah, was Adel's oldest half sister. In the local culture, if the oldest child is a girl, a slight change is made to her father's name and his altered name is given to her. In Hind's case, her (and Adel's) father's name was Majid, so she was called Mujudah.

hookah

(English) also known as shisha or hubbly-bubbly, a single- or multi-stemmed water pipe, usually made of glass, used for heating or vaporizing and then smoking either tobacco, hashish, or opium.

Hussein - حسين

(Arabic) Adel's older half brother.

Isha - صلاة العشاء

(Arabic) one of the five mandatory Islamic prayers. Isha is the second prayer of the day—the night prayer—as the Islamic day starts at sunset. If counted from midnight, it is the fifth prayer of the day.

kal kidan - ቃል ኪዳን

(Amharic) a type of marriage in Ethiopia that is based on a civil contract.

kebele - ቀበሌ

(Amharic) neighborhood or ward; the smallest administrative unit of Ethiopia.

Kebur Zabagna - ክቡር ዘበኛ

(Amharic) the Ethiopian Imperial/Honor Guard, also known as the First Division.

King Dhu Nuwas - الملك ذو نواس-

(Arabic) a Jewish Himyarite king.

King Ezana - ዒዛና
(Geʿez/Amharic) the Aksumite king who established Christianity in Ethiopia.

King Kaleb - ንጉስ ካሌብ
(Geʿez/Amharic) the Aksumite king who invaded Yemen (South Arabia) in 524 AD.

Lake Tana - ጣና ሀይቅ
Lake Tana is Ethiopia's largest lake. It is the source of the Blue Nile and is therefore of great significance to all Ethiopians. It was formed about five million years ago due to volcanic activity in the area—what is now an Amhara region in the northwestern Ethiopian Highlands. A dam controls the flow of water into the Blue Nile from Lake Tana, so the depth of the lake fluctuates with the release of water into the Nile and the impact of rainfall. Lake Tana is approximately eighty-four kilometers (fifty-two miles) long and sixty-six kilometers (forty-one miles) wide. Its maximum depth is fifteen meters (forty-nine-feet).[5]

listro (slang) - ሊስትሮ
(Amharic/Italian) a boy who works as a shoeshine. Shoe shiner or boot polisher is an occupation in which a person cleans and buffs shoes and then applies a waxy paste to give a shiny appearance and a protective coating.

lustrascarpe
(Italian) a shoe shiner.

Maekelawi - ማዕከላዊ እስር ቤት
Maekelawi is an infamous jail in Addis Ababa that has long been synonymous with abuse and repression. It stopped being operational in 2018. Many who were incarcerated in Maekelawi were political prisoners, arrested for their

perceived political views. The public was largely unaware of the existence of Maekelawi much less the fate of those who were imprisoned there. Today, Maekelawi is open to the public as a museum.

Maghrib/Maghreb - صلاة المغرب
(Arabic) sunset prayer; one of the five mandatory Islamic prayers. Because an Islamic day starts at sunset, the Maghrib prayer is the first prayer of the day. If counted from midnight, it is the fourth prayer of the day.

Majid - ماجد
(Arabic) Adel's father.

Mamecha - ማመጭ ማንደፍሮ
(Amharic) Emebet's husband.

mancala
(English) a family of two-player, turn-based strategy board games played with small stones, beans, or seeds and rows of holes or pits in the earth, a board or other playing surface. The objective is usually to capture all or some of the opponent's pieces.

Manella Carmel
(Italian) Adel's childhood classmate and first crush.

Maryam Afif - مريم عفيف
(Arabic) one of Adel's Yemeni stepmothers.

Matias - ማትያስ
(Amharic) one of Adel's childhood friends. Matias and Adel attended evangelical Sunday school together for approximately nine months.

Mengistu Haile Mariam - መንግስቱ ኃይለማሪያም
(Amharic) president of Ethiopia from 1977-1991.

Meseret - መሰረት

(Amharic) one of Adel's cousins. Daughter of Emebet and Mamecha; sister to Getahun.

Meskerem - መስከረም

(Amharic) the Ethiopian month occurring September 11-October 10. Meskerem marks the beginning of the Ethiopian year.

Mesopotamia

Mesopotamia today includes most of Iraq, Kuwait, Iran, Syria, and Turkey. It is the historical region of Western Asia at the head of the Persian Gulf near the Tigris-Euphrates River system.

Metehara/Matahara

a town in the East Shewa zone of the Oromia state of central Ethiopia, where Adel's father unexpectedly died and was buried.

Muna - منى / ሙና

(Arabic) one of Adel's half sisters.

Muwalladin - مولدين

(Arabic) a person of mixed race, specifically one who has one parent of Arab descent and one non-Arab parent.

Nadia Basherahil - نادية باشراحيل

(Arabic) the child Weinishet nannied when she met Adel's father and became pregnant with Adel.

Nazreth

a city of approximately 325,000, now known officially as Adaamaa or Adama; not to be confused with Nazareth in Israel.

Oromia
Oromia, homeland of the Oromo people, is a regional state in central Ethiopia. Addis Ababa, the capital city of Ethiopia, is in Oromia.

Prophet Muhammed (peace be upon him/pbuh)
(Arabic) the Arab social, political, and religious leader who founded Islam.

Qur'an - القرآن
(Arabic/English) the main religious text of Islam, believed by Muslims to be a revelation from God (Allah). It is widely regarded as the finest work in classical Arabic literature.

qurban - ቁርባን
(Amharic) the most prestigious and the most sacred type of marriage in Ethiopia; qurban marriages cannot be dissolved.

Ramadan - رمضان
a period of one month of fasting, prayer, reflection, and community. During this month, Muslims are prohibited from eating, drinking, smoking, or engaging in sexual activity from dawn to dusk. It takes place during the ninth month of the Hijiri calendar and is observed by Muslims worldwide. The end of Ramadan is marked by Eid, a celebration involving feasts. The Gregorian calendar is eleven days longer than the Hijiri calendar, which is based on the motion of the moon and is composed of twelve months of 29.5 days. Therefore, Ramadan is on different dates on the Gregorian calendar each year.

Rukia Atufa - رقية عطوفة
(Arabic) the stepmother who raised Adel until Adel's father's death.

salat - صالات
(Arabic) the obligatory Muslim prayers, performed five times each day; the second Pillar of Islam.

Salem Bagarsh - سليم باجريش
(Arabic) Adel's father's friend. Along with Bansser and Baobaid, Bagarsh played a major role supporting Adel during his first sixteen years in Ethiopia. He was instrumental in getting Adel a South Yemeni passport and sending him to North Yemen.

Sanford International School Kebena
a British school that was established in the 1940s in Addis Ababa when Mrs. Christine Sandford, the wife of Colonel Sandford, Head of the British Military Mission to Ethiopia during World War II, wanted an English-speaking school for her children. It is the school Adel's half brother, Hussein, attended.

sawm - صوم
(Arabic) One of the Five Pillars of Islam, sawm is fasting, which Muslims are expected to do from sunrise to sunset during Ramadan.

Shabbat - שבת
(Hebrew) Shabbat means "he rested," and refers to the seventh day after creation, the day of rest.

Shahada - الشهادة
(Arabic) an Islamic oath, with the literal meaning "faith"; one of the Five Pillars of Islam.

Sheikha - شيخة
(Arabic) one of Adel's half sisters.

Shewa Robit
Shewa Robit is a town in north-central Ethiopia and is the birthplace of Adel's mother. Ethiopia's largest jail is in this town.

shisha/sheesha - شيشة
(Arabic/English) a single- or multi-stemmed water pipe, usually made of glass, used for heating or vaporizing and then smoking either tobacco, hashish, or opium; also known as hookah or hubbly-bubbly.

Sodere
a spa town in central Ethiopia approximately 120 kilometers (seventy-six miles) southeast of Addis Ababa and twenty-five kilometers (sixteen miles) south of Nazreth. It features lush, shady vegetation, and the hot springs minutes out of the town are popular for their therapeutic effects.

Tahasas - ታኅሳስ
(Amharic) the month of the Ethiopian calendar that coincides with December 10-January 8 in the Gregorian calendar.

Tanakh - תנ״ך
(Hebrew) the Hebrew Bible; the book of Hebrew scriptures including the Torah, the Nevi'im, and the Ketuvim.

Tilahun Gesses - ጥላሁን ገሠሠ
(Amharic) a male Ethiopian singer popular in the 1960s and 70s.

Timket/Timkat - ጥምቀት
(Amharic) The Ethiopian Orthodox celebration of Epiphany on January 19 (January 20 in a leap year) is one of the most celebrated events in the Ethiopian calendar; from the Ge'ez word ateryo, which means "to reveal."

Torah - תּוֹרָה
(Hebrew) the first five books of the Hebrew Bible: Genesis, Exodus, Leviticus, Numbers, and Deuteronomy—the five Books of Moses; known in the Jewish tradition as the written Torah.

Ustaz Basherahil - سيد بشراهيل
(Arabic) the Arabic teacher who thought Adel the Arabic language and the Islamic religion from 1967-1970.

Weinishet Fertewehal; Weinishet Fertewehal Tachbele -
ወይንሸት ፈርተወሀል ታችበሌ
(Amharic) Adel's biological mother.

Wudu - الوضوء
(Arabic) a minor ablution in Islam. Muslims cleanse parts of their bodies: face, arms, head, and then feet.

Yenat Fanta - የናት ፋንታ
(Amharic) a name that means "a reward of a mother who passed away."

Zakat - زينب
(Arabic) the giving of alms; one of the Five Pillars of Islam; a religious duty for all Muslims who are financially able to help the needy.

Zeinab Afif
(Arabic) one of Adel's stepmothers. Cousin to Maryam, another of Adel's stepmothers, Zeinab was married to Adel's father (Majid) when Majid had an affair with Maryam.

Appendices

The following four appendices have been included to provide additional historical, cultural, and religious information about Ethiopia.

Appendix One The Kingdom of Aksum: This appendix provides information on how Christianity came to Ethiopia. Because of the religious instruction I received as a child and the significance of religion (particularly the Ark of Covenant) in Ethiopia, I wanted offer up more historical and religious context than I could get into in the main body of the book.

Appendix Two WW II and the Abyssinian Campaigns: information about the political history of Ethiopia, the only African country to have not been colonized by Europeans. I've provided this background to show how my father was involved in the military and how he came to reside in Ethiopia.

Appendix Three Meskel Square: Most major cities have a central square or gathering place that is used for political demonstrations but also celebrations. Meskel Square in Addis Ababa is significant because of its use throughout history in both revolutions and religious festivals. I've provided information about Meskel Square as it was a main gathering place during the 1970s Ethiopian Revolution.

Appendix Four My Observations of Ethiopia in Recent Years: I was sixteen years old when I moved from Ethiopia to North Yemen. I have not lived in Ethiopia since, but I regularly visit my family there. It's interesting to see how the culture and landscape change. I've recorded my observations of changes in the country over the past several decades.

Appendix One

The Kingdom of Aksum

By the 400s BC, a distinct Ethiopian culture with city states was starting to develop, and the peoples of this region began to vie for power and control over trade routes. The ancient Kingdom of Aksum emerged in northern Ethiopia and Eritrea and remained in power from approximately 80 BC to 825 AD, with its power reaching its height in the third and fourth centuries AD. Due to its location along the Red Sea, Aksum quickly gained control over trade along the commercial route between the Roman Empire and ancient India, establishing East Africa as the hub of trade between Africa and Asia.

The Aksumite rulers maintained their control of trade by becoming one of the earliest states in Africa to mint its own currency, which they used in trade with Rome, Persia, North Africa, and Asia, the other powerful regions at the time. Archaeologists believe that silver coins were used internally because of inscriptions in Ge'ez on the silver coins that have been discovered in the area, but the Aksumites minted other currency that was used outside of the kingdom, as well. Gold, being much more valuable than silver, was used by the elite, who didn't trade at the smaller level that lower-level merchants did.[1] The Aksumites produced their own pottery but also imported pottery and other exotic items from other lands. Their access to frankincense, gold, and myrrh gave the Aksumites the upper hand, as these items were desired by their trade partners.[2]

The Aksumites also established and maintained a strong political and military presence in the Arabian Peninsula and eventually extended their rule over the region with the conquest of the Himyarite Kingdom. Between 183-213 AD, they crossed the Red Sea and invaded South Arabia (what is now Yemen), conquering and inhabiting the coastal lands of the Sabeans. They ruled that area for half a century in the sixth century.

The Aksumites erected monumental obelisks, which served a religious purpose in pre-Christian times. The obelisks, which were erected in the third and fourth centuries, marked graves and also represented and honored the rulers of the time. Stones were chiseled from the nearby mountains, moved by elephants, and used for making the monuments.3 The stele from King Ezana is believed to have been the last one erected.4

King Kaleb sent an army to North Yemen around 525 AD to fight against the Jewish Himyarite King Dhu Nuwas because of the persecution of Christians there. "Dhu Nuwas was deposed and killed, and Kaleb appointed a Christian Himyarite, Esimiphaios ('Sumuafa Ashawa'), as his viceroy."5

However, the Aksumite general Abraha, with assistance from Ethiopians who had settled in North Yemen, overthrew this viceroy in 530 AD. Kaleb twice resisted and fought against Abraha but was defeated both times. After the second defeat, Kaleb relented and recognized Abraha as his new viceroy.

The next fifty years saw multiple additional conflicts in the area (the Aksumite-Persian wars),6 culminating with the siege of Sana'a, capital of Aksumite Yemen. "In 575, the wars resumed again ... These wars may have been Aksum's swansong as a great power, with an overall weakening of Aksumite authority and over-expenditure in money and manpower."7

The Ethiopian Orthodox Church

Religion and trade were the two most important aspects of life in the Aksumite Kingdom. The city of Aksum, one of the oldest cities in Africa, was the birthplace of Christianity in Ethiopia.

King Ezana of Axum was a powerful ruler, controlling both sides of the Red Sea. In the middle of the fourth century, Byzantine priests arrived in Aksum to spread the Christian faith. In 350 AD, King Ezana was converted to Christianity, and Christianity became the official religion of Aksum. King Ezana is therefore credited with bringing Christianity to Ethiopia. Christianity began to spread in the area because it was followed by the elite. The Byzantine monks continued to travel further inland, spreading the gospel by teaching, writing books, and translating Christian teachings from other languages.8

The Axumite Kingdom continued to be a controlling force in the region until the rise of Islam in other regions began to disconnect Aksum from other countries. The Aksumites began to lose their influence in the seventh century; the shift in religious, economic, and ecological power in the area led to the decline of the Aksum empire.9

The Ark of the Covenant

The Ark of the Covenant is the gold-covered wooden chest mentioned in the Book of Exodus in which the two stone tablets of the Ten Commandments were stored:

> *They shall make an ark of acacia wood. Two cubits and a half shall be its length, a cubit and a half its breadth, and a cubit and a half its height. You shall overlay it with pure gold, inside and outside shall you overlay it, and you shall make on it a molding of gold around it. You shall cast four rings of gold for it and put them on its four feet, two rings on the one side of it, and two rings on the other side of it. You shall make poles of acacia wood and overlay them with gold. And you shall put the poles into the rings on the sides of the ark to carry the ark by them. The poles shall remain in the rings of the ark; they shall not be taken from it. And you shall put into the ark the testimony that I shall give you.*
>
> *You shall make a mercy seat of pure gold. Two cubits and a half shall be its length, and a cubit and a half its breadth. And you shall make two cherubim of gold; of hammered work shall you make them, on the two ends of the mercy seat. Make one cherub on the one end, and one cherub on the other end. Of one piece with the mercy seat shall you make the cherubim on its two ends. The cherubim shall spread out their wings above, overshadowing the mercy seat with their wings, their faces one to another; toward the mercy seat shall the faces of the cherubim be. And you shall put the mercy seat on the top of the ark, and in the ark you shall put the testimony that I shall give you (Exodus 25:10-21).*

According to the New Testament Book of Hebrews, it also contained Aaron's rod and a pot of manna: "having the golden altar of incense and the Ark of the Covenant covered on all sides with gold, in which was a golden urn holding the manna, and Aaron's staff that budded, and the tablets of the covenant" (Hebrews 9:4).

The Ethiopian Orthodox Church claims that the original Ark of the Covenant is currently kept in the Treasury of the Church of Our Lady Mary of Zion, the building next to the Church of Our Lady Mary of Zion in Axum. The Treasury has a designated guard, a monk who never leaves the property.

Every Ethiopian Orthodox Church contains a wooden replica of the ark. These replicas of the ark are considered the most holy item in the churches.

The Kebra Nagast (The Glory of the Kings) is a fourteenth-century book written in Ge'ez telling the story of how the Queen of Sheba and King Solomon met and how the real Ark of the Covenant was brought to Ethiopia by their son, Menelik the First. This document also claims that a forgery of the ark was left in the Temple in Jerusalem.10 Ethiopians accept the Kebra Nagast as historical fact. Menelik the First became the first ruler of the Axumite Kingdom.

The Queen of Sheba had traveled from the Axum region to visit King Solomon with gold, spices, and precious stones. She was intelligent and forward thinking, and she wanted to learn Solomon's wisdom. "Now when the Queen of Sheba heard of the fame of Solomon concerning the name of the Lord, she came to test him with hard questions" (1 Kings 10:1).

The Dungur Palace in Aksum city is believed to be the Palace of the Queen of Sheba.

Appendix Two

WW II and the Abyssinian Campaigns

Within the past hundred and fifty years, Italy twice tried to invade and take control over Ethiopia—on March 1, 1896 and October 3, 1935—and twice they failed. The Italians were, in fact, the first European power to be defeated by Africa, and to this day, Ethiopia is the only country in Africa that has not been colonized.

The European colonial representatives invaded African nations with misconceptions of the local realities. Ethiopians believed they were equal to, if not better than, the Europeans when it came to self-pride, dignity, and territorialism. Italy was committed to giving land to Italian settlers in Ethiopia, which spawned animosity toward and distrust of foreign rulers within the Ethiopian people. What the Italians didn't know was that, unlike many other African countries, Ethiopia had a civilization as old as 2,000 years with a written language and a defined culture and religion. Ethiopia also possessed a developed human network between tribes through which they could communicate and therefore promote the defense of the boundaries of their country. To not recognize these factors was a major misjudgment on the part of the Italians.

The initial defeat of the Italian army is one of the greatest battles in the history of Africa—the Battle of Adwa, which ended the first Italo-Ethiopian War.[1] As a result of the Battle of Adwa, Ethiopia became a global symbol of freedom for Black people.

The prospect of war between the two countries increased dramatically again after Mussolini took control of Italy in 1922. He sought Ethiopia for its resources but also to salvage the pride of the only European nation defeated by an African country.

Taking Ethiopia would have also completed the Italian domination over the Horn of Africa. At that time, Italy had colonial forces in neighboring Eritrea and Somalia.

In the 1930s, almost forty years after the first defeat, Mussolini sought control over Ethiopia as an opportunity to provide land for unemployed Italians. During the Great Depression, Mussolini wanted to distract his people with his overseas successes and open up new opportunities for Italy; he aimed to acquire more mineral resources to fight off the effects of the Great Depression. In 1931, Italy had invaded Abyssinia without any declarations of war, but in 1935, the Italians again invaded Abyssinia because they were unsatisfied with their rewards after World War I.

Despite historical internal differences, Ethiopians regrouped to defend themselves. As was done in the past, the sitting king personally directed the battle front; this time it was the role of Haile Selassie to personally campaign against the Italian troops in northern Abyssinia, but the better equipped Italian troops, coupled with their willingness to deploy chemical weapons, frustrated the Abyssinian Emperor, forcing him into exile during World War II. While in exile, he appealed to the League of Nations and was known to be one of the first African leaders to become a figure on the global stage.

As WW II progressed on the European continent, and as the balance of the war tilted, it was necessary for the British Empire to claim territories that were under German and Italian control in North and East Africa.

The East African campaign (also known as the Abyssinian campaign) was fought in East Africa during the Second World War by Allies of WW II, mainly from the British Empire, against Italy and its colony of Italian East Africa, between June 1940 and November 1941.

> *The British Middle East Command with troops from the*
> *United Kingdom, South Africa, British India, Uganda*
> *Protectorate, Kenya, Somaliland, West Africa, Northern*
> *and Southern Rhodesia, Sudan, and Nyasaland*
> *participated in the campaign. These were joined by the*
> *Allied Force Publique of Belgian Congo, Imperial*
> *Ethiopian Arbegnoch (resistance forces) and a small unit*
> *of Free French.*[2]

In September 1939, Great Britain declared war on Italy. A year and a half later, on April 6, 1941, British and Ethiopian troops drove the Italians out of Addis Abba and re-established Emperor Haile Selassie as head of the Ethiopian government. Ethiopia was the first nation liberated from Axis powers in WW II.

My Father's Role in the British Military

Two million Arabs and Indians fought for the British in WW II. My father was one of those soldiers.

The British selected desired Arabs based on their stature (my father was a foreboding six feet or 182 centimeters tall), their language skills (my father spoke Arabic, Italian, and English), and other skills. My father could shoot, drive, and translate, so he was useful to the British. From the age of twenty, he was on contract with the British military for three years. After working on a contract basis, at the age of twenty-three, he joined them full time in 1935, at the time of increasing tensions between the Ethiopians and Italians, and served for an additional ten years.

My father was part of the British Forces Aden, which was the name given to the British Armed Forces stationed in the Aden Protectorate (in South Yemen) in the middle of the twentieth century. "Their purpose was to preserve the security of the Protectorate from both internal threats and external aggression."[3]

In the spring of 1941, his division was instrumental in ultimately thwarting that second attempt by Italy to take control over Ethiopia. A detailed account of the final battle is found in Chapter 18 of *East African and Abyssinian Campaigns*, by Neil Orpen. The two-month-long battle involved hand-to-hand combat, blowing up bridges, air strikes, and round-the-clock artillery battles, culminating with the surrender of Addis Ababa by the Italians.

> *Escorted by motorcycle police, General Mambrini,*
> *Inspector-General of the Italian East African Police, drove*
> *out with a white flag to meet the advance guard of the*
> *King's African Rifles and surrendered the city, in which he*
> *feared for the lives of Italian troops and civilians alike ...*
> *The King's African Rifles had won the race for Addis*
> *Ababa.*[4]

This two-month long battle would have surely been an intense experience for my father. And who knows what else he saw and did in his ten years serving the British?

Upon his retirement from the British military, my father settled in Ethiopia, turning his attention to becoming a businessman. Had my father not been in the British Army and fought in WW II, he wouldn't have been living in Ethiopia in the 1960s. And I would not have been born.

As I started piecing together details of my father's life, I came to learn how alcohol and cigarettes were used as currency in the military and how alcoholism and post-traumatic stress disorder (PTSD) were contributing factors to not only his untimely death but also the lifestyle he developed in his last twenty years. Due to British influence, he brought with him new habits such as the way he dressed, eating with cutlery, and his penchant for indulging in alcohol and cigarettes. These habits, his hobbies such as hunting and camping, and his handwriting and drawing abilities differentiated and ultimately alienated him from his fellow Arabs. To his Arab (Muslim) peers, his drinking was shameful—a horrible sin. The Arabs saw the result of my father's time in the military—his foreign habits and particularly his drinking—but did not understand the factors that contributed to him having adopted these traits.

Soldiers and PTSD

I learned that in my father's division, the soldiers were given rum to encourage them to fight. I can't say so with any certainty, but it is likely that this is where my father's problems with alcohol stemmed from. He was surely one of thousands, if not hundreds of thousands, of men who emerged from WW II with addictions to alcohol and tobacco. Add to that the fact that in the British military, Arab and Indian soldiers were not treated with as much esteem as those hailing from the UK. Racism and segregation were constants. I have heard many reports that Indian soldiers in particular received lower payment and inferior living accommodations than the British soldiers.

Alcoholism is not a problem that gets left behind on the battlefield. It goes hand in hand with PTSD. According to the Mayo Clinic, "self-destructive behavior, such as drinking too much or driving too fast"[5] is one of many ways PTSD sufferers seek to escape from their nightmares, flashbacks, depression, and anxiety. Unfortunately, the use of alcohol is counterproductive as "alcohol can exacerbate feelings of depression and other dangerous symptoms that can lead to suicide or otherwise put an individual's life in danger."[6]

It has only been in the past twenty to thirty years that we, in Canada and the US, have begun to acknowledge the impact that PTSD has on those who have served in combat. "In 1994, no one saw post-traumatic stress disorder (PTSD) for what it was. [Roméo] Dallaire learned soon enough that hard work wouldn't make it go away."[7] In his book, *Waiting for First Light: My Ongoing Battle with PTSD*, Dallaire, the former lieutenant-general who led Canada's peacekeeping mission in Rwanda in the 1990s, opened up about his long-term battles with PTSD, emphasizing that more than twenty years after his first-hand experience witnessing the genocide in Rwanda, he still struggles with depression, flashbacks, nightmares, extreme emotional responses to triggering events, and more.

> *Canadians became widely aware that Dallaire had not, could not, leave the slaughter behind in June 2000, when it was widely reported he had been found near-comatose from a mix of scotch and anti-depressants beneath a park bench near his Hull [Québec] home. (He twice asked the ambulance crew to kill him.)[8]*

And this is why I say that my father was misunderstood. If we, in Western society, have only made strides in the past two or three decades to begin to acknowledge the impact of PTSD on soldiers, certainly my father would not have been recognized in South Yemen or in Africa as struggling with what comes along with PTSD: emotional outbursts, the abuse of alcohol and cigarettes, and so on. Arabs of that generation had no understanding of PTSD. He was labeled as a "bad apple," and judged for being temperamental or hot-headed and for his misuse of alcohol. Other Arabs saw his behavior as a character flaw rather than a mental health issue.

Certainly he was difficult to live with, as some of my stepmothers have attested to. As Dallaire points out, family members also suffer the consequences of PTSD when soldiers return home after combat mission, but their suffering is often overshadowed by the struggles the returning soldiers face.[9] Not to excuse my father's behavior, but his beating of his maids, drivers, and guards; losing his temper with his wives; and his alcoholism were undoubtedly largely due to PTSD. The conditioning of ten years of active service in the military during WW II and the sudden, horrible incident in which he shot and killed his own friend in a hunting accident surely left him to deal with similar PTSD-related issues that other soldiers of his generation—Canadian, German, British, American, Dutch, French, etc.—would have been left with. In the 1940s, 50s, and 60s, though, no one talked about PTSD, even in Western countries. Possessing no understanding of PTSD, and certainly offering no help for those who suffered from it, his culture left him to try to maneuver through and manage his internal torment, which certainly explains some of his self-destructive behavior in his last years.

In Arab culture, drinking is looked upon as taboo. My father was guilty of defying his cultural norms. However, how many of us in any society take part in activities which we hide from our peers or even our own family members? In any culture, there is a certain degree of hypocrisy and inconsistency between what people claim to believe versus how they actually conduct themselves. And the reasons behind our actions may be deeply hidden or unacknowledged if others don't understand and especially don't *want* to understand an individual's behavior.

If Dallaire, with the help of medication and other psychological supports and treatments that are available today, still struggles with managing PTSD, my father, left untreated and even undiagnosed, was surely fighting a difficult and perhaps, at times, seemingly hopeless internal battle. Perhaps our societies have a long way to go to better support those we call our war heroes and to understand each other in general.

Campaign Medals

My father was awarded the following medals for his military service:

War Medal 1939-1945

As with most Armed Forces personnel serving during the conflict of World War II, he was entitled to the War Medal 1939-1945. This medal was awarded to all full-time service personnel who had completed twenty-eight days of service between September 3, 1939 and September 2, 1945.

1939-45 Star

My father was awarded the 1939-45 Star for operational service in WW II between September 3, 1939 and September 2, 1945.

Italy Star

The Italy Star was a campaign medal awarded to my father and other soldiers of the British Commonwealth for service in World War II. This medal was awarded for operational service in Sicily or Italy during the period June 1, 1943 and May 8, 1945.

Please visit adelbenharhara.com/gallery to view pictures of these medals.

Appendix Three

Meskel Square

Meskel Square is an important gathering place in Addis Ababa and has been used for centuries for political, social, and cultural assemblies and demonstrations including concerts, parades, and political rallies.

Meskel means cross, and the Meskel Festival, which has been an annual celebration for more than 1,600 years, "commemorates the moment when the [location of the] crucifix was revealed to Empress Helena of Constantinople, mother of Constantine the Great."[1] The festival takes place beginning on the evening of September 26 every year, which is *Meskerem* 17 on the Ethiopian calendar. During the festival, thousands gather with torches, which they use to light a *Demera* (pyramid), which "is located in the center and is circled by priests in brightly colored cloaks, students, brass bands, and the army carrying around giant crosses and torches."[2] Traditionally, the pyramid was lit by the Emperor of Ethiopia as well as high officials of the Orthodox Church and government, members of the Imperial family, and other nobility.[3] The smoke from the bonfire was rumored to show Helena (Queen Eleni) the burial location of the True Cross of Jesus.[4] The pyramid burns throughout the night until dawn, when the celebrations end.

The square was renamed *Abyot* (Revolution Square) in 1974 when the government fell and communism took hold.

It was greatly expanded so that it could accommodate the annual Revolution Day and May Day parades on September 12 and May 1. Three gigantic portraits of Karl

> *Marx, Friedrich Engels, and Vladimir Lenin were erected*
> *in the square. The population of Addis Ababa would joke*
> *that these were the "new trinity."[5]*

In 1988, the government ordered that the bonfire be moved to a smaller square located outside the southern gates of St. George Cathedral. However,

> *after the fall of Mengistu Haile Mariam [in 1991], the*
> *short-lived government of General Tesfaye Gebre Kidan*
> *restored the original name of Meskel Square, and the*
> *Ethiopian People's Revolutionary Democratic Front*
> *government returned the Meskel celebration to the square.[6]*

At the east entrance to the square, visitors will find a national monument built to honor those who were massacred in the 1970s during the Red Terror. The Red Terror Martyrs' Memorial Museum, located at the edge of the square, opened in February 2010.[7]

These days, the square is still used for political demonstrations, rallies, and protests, such as the one in August 2016, when hundreds of protesters demonstrated, shouting, "We want our freedom!" and "Free our political prisoners!"[8]

Appendix Four

My Observations of Ethiopia in Recent Years

During my visits to Ethiopia in 2010 and 2020, it was difficult for me not to compare the country to how it was during in the 1960s and 1970s. In my youth, many people walked barefoot and wore traditional, locally made clothing. The streets were less crowded and cleaner, the majority of people consumed homemade alcoholic beverages, and often people ate at home. It was particularly shameful for women to eat out. Therefore, there were fewer restaurants. Shops and businesses bore local names, such as names of historical sites or individual Ethiopian names. I only ever heard people asking others their place of birth, as people were identified by birthplace rather than ethnicity. Although the educated population was smaller in size, even a high school student was aware of what was transpiring around the globe. Moreover, other than during the revolution, none were thinking to leave their homeland, and people always took pride in being Ethiopian with its rich culture and history and being a symbol of Africa and the Black race.

In my recent visits, however, two-thirds of the businesses, including hotels, were named after foreign cities. I asked why. The answer I was given was that foreign and in particular American-sounding names attracted more clientele, especially tourists. I was astonished to witness the long lineups in mini malls to eat pizza or hamburgers. While the Western world is slowly turning away from fast-food chains and aiming to adopt a healthier lifestyle, Ethiopia seems to be headed in the opposite direction. I was perplexed, wondering why a culture that had always been so healthy was now emulating Western bad habits.

Almost everyone was wearing shoes and Western outfits made in China, exposing the change in body mass from lean-looking Ethiopians I used to know to disproportional body shapes such as large buttocks, a big belly, and skinny legs. The change in body shapes is surely because of the influence of fast food. The most visible changes that slapped me in the face were the number of women wearing weaves or hair extensions and low-rise jeans to reveal their G-string underwear (the "whale tail") and boys wearing trousers or jeans that sag so low that the top of the trousers or jeans is significantly below the waist, sometimes revealing much of the wearer's underpants.

I was introduced to the sagging style of pants when I was living in the US during the early 1990s. Other than thinking it was a bit distasteful, I didn't concern myself much with this trend. Someone who thought that I was judgmental told me that it was a symbol of freedom and cultural awareness among some youths or a symbol of their rejection of the values of mainstream society. In fact, that person claimed the style had originated in the American jail system, where belts are sometimes prohibited and there can be a lack of appropriately sized clothing. Anything is possible in the US, but I was unable to grasp why Ethiopians were adopting this style.

The Ethiopia I knew was a nation of multiple languages, ethnicities, and religions. I grew up in a multicultural community where no one asked which tribe or ethnicity one belonged to. In fact, the first time I was exposed to tribal and primitive thinking was when I moved to North Yemen. Until recently, I was not aware of my mother's ethnicity, and I had to phone my cousin Sahle, who lives in Atlanta, Georgia, to enlighten me about my race on my mother's side.

When I was still coming to terms with the notion of my father having been buried outside both the Muslim and Christian cemeteries, I recently learned of the existence of areas within

Ethiopia where a member of one faith group is not allowed to build a place of worship and/or where individuals of a certain faith are not allowed to be buried. I'm wondering if the human race has made any progress emotionally and spiritually since the stone age.

Apparently, Ethiopians have divided up the nation into elements of ethnicity, and borders are drawn based on ethnicity (as they call it, ethnic federalism); that is what continues to prompt war and conflict. The US and Canada have states and provinces, but they are not divided based on ethnicity. The boundaries between states are invisible, and the federal system and local administrative units co-exist while applying law and order. However, Ethiopia is now divided on ethnic lines; pockets of people from specific ethnicities are concentrated in certain areas. The attitudes have changed to "this is our area; that is your area." The borders are political, and if people cross over into a different group's territory, conflict arises. People want to do business in different locations, but because of territorialism, there is resistance. It's a recipe for disaster as each group clings to their own ideas and practices and aims to choke out the other.

From my reading and growing awareness, the colonial system worldwide divided nations without giving any consideration to the natives who occupied the lands. The world hasn't fully healed from such miscalculations and mismanagement. While societies suffered from the syndrome of the last major war (WW II), the UN went on to create two nations purely based on religion (Israel and Pakistan). Any level-headed person can see what is transpiring between Arabs and Israelis or between India and Pakistan. I thought, *This is a recipe to start a long-lasting dog fight in Ethiopia, too.*

My stance on socialism today has also changed over the years. I'm not fond of the extreme type of communism or socialism that I was supporting as a teen in the 1970s. I prefer the type of social and economic structure I see in Scandinavian countries and Canada, too. Health care is a human right. Balanced social services are necessary. I don't think I would want to live in the US again, nor am I fond of the extreme version of the capitalism they are applying.

But these are just my personal musings at this point in my life, as a sixty-year-old man in 2022.

Bibliography

Angela. "10 Symptoms of PTSD." *Facty Health*. Updated May 21, 2019.
    facty.com/conditions/ptsd/10-symptoms-of-ptsd/?.

ANU Museum of the Jewish People. "The Jewish Community of Ethiopia."
    The Museum of the Jewish People. 1996.
    dbs.anumuseum.org.il/skn/en/c6/e195130/Place/Ethiopia

BBC News Africa. "The Rise of Aksum—History of Africa with Zienab
    Badawi [Episode 5]." YouTube Video, 44:48. April 19, 2020.
    youtube.com/watch?v=A4OSEpexs_Q.

Bethune, Brian. "Inside Roméo Dallaire's Ongoing Battle with PTSD."
    MACLEAN'S. October 21, 2016.
    macleans.ca/culture/books/inside-romeo-dallaires-brutally-
    revealing-new-memoir/.

BililaAward.org. "Abebe Bikila." Accessed December 27, 2021.
    bikilaaward.org/about_us/bikila/index.html.

Insight Ethiopia. "Episode 15: Axumite Kingdom: The Rise and Fall of an
    Empire." December 4, 2013. YouTubeVideo, 27:48. youtube/ad-
    k2nwJGZw.

"How to Celebrate the Ethopian New Year." Absolute Ethiopia Tours.
    Accessed December 3, 2021. absoluteethiopia.com/how-to-
    celebrate-the-ethiopian-new-year/.

Kloman, Harry. "Setting the Ethiopian Table," Ethiopian Food: Mesob
    Across America. April 1, 2013, 8:04 a.m.
    ethiopianfood.wordpress.com/2013/04/01/setting-the-ethiopian-
    table/.

"Meskel Festival: Finding of the True Cross." *WATA*. 2021. wata-
    dmc.net/dmc/travel-fit-products/ethiopia/meskel-festival-finding-
    of-the-true-cross/.

Nilsondm. "Abebe Bikila." December 3, 2012. YouTube Video, 22:50.
    youtube.com/watch?v=9FC8ozQtTEk.

Orpen, Neil. *South African Forces World War II: East African and Abyssinian
    Campaigns*. October 1968, p 250.
    hibiblio.org/hyperwar/UN/SouthAfrica/EAfrica/EAfrica-18.html

"Post-Traumatic Stress Disorder (PTSD)." Mayo Clinic, 2021.
    mayoclinic.org/diseases-conditions/post-traumatic-stress-
    disorder/symptoms-causes/syc-20355967.

"Red Terror Martyrs Memorial Museum.*"MOMAA | African Modern Online
    Art Gallery & Lifestyle*. 2021. momaa.org/directory/red-terror-
    martyrs-memorial-museum/.

Bibliography

Senna, Danzy. *New People*. New York: Penguin Random House, 2017. p. 114 of 281. Adobe Digital Editions EPUB.

Shaikh, Ahmed. "Islamic Inheritance: A Guide for American Muslims." *IslamicInheritance.com*. accessed November 30, 2021. islamicinheritance.com/islamic-inheritance-guide/

"Truth to Power: The Book of Esther." Ministry Pass, 2021. ministrypass.com/resource/truth-to-power-the-book-of-esther/

2007 Wikipedia Selection for Schools. "Code of Hammurabi." Accessed December 19, 2021. cs.mcgill.ca/~rwest/wikispeedia/wpcd/wp/c/Code_of_Hammurabi.htm.

Ubelacker, Sheryl. "Romeo Dallaire's Memoir Sheds Light on Former Canadian General's Battle with PTSD." CTV NEWS. Last updated Friday October 28, 2016. ctvnews.ca/health/romeo-dallaire-memoir-sheds-light-on-former-canadian-general-s-battle-with-ptsd-1.3135585.

"What is Ta`awwudh and Tasmiyah?" *Sabiqoon Blog Space*. December 16, 2012. alsabiqoon.blogspot.com/2012/12/what-is-taawwudh-and-tasmiyah.html.

"What Was the Significance of Jesus Washing the Feet of the Disciples?" Got Questions Ministries. accessed December 16, 2021. gotquestions.org/Jesus-washing-feet.html.

"Wikipedia: 1960 Ethiopian coup d'état attempt." Wikimedia Foundation. Last edited October 5, 2021, 08:06. en.wikipedia.org/wiki/1960_Ethiopian_coup_d%27%C3%A9tat_attempt.

"Wikipedia: Ād." Wikimedia Foundation." Last edited November 18, 2021, 17:28. en.wikipedia.org/wiki/%CA%BF%C4%80d - Legend.

"Wikipedia: Agaw people." Wikimedia Foundation. Last edited November 7, 2021, 18:42. en.wikipedia.org/wiki/Agaw_people.

"Wikipedia: Arabic." Wikimedia Foundation. Last edited November 29, 2021, 12:33. en.wikipedia.org/wiki/Arabic.

"Wikipedia: Ark of the Covenant." Wikimedia Foundation. Last edited December 2, 2021, 01:59. en.wikipedia.org/wiki/Ark_of_the_Covenant.

"Wikipedia: Battle of Adwa." Wikimedia Foundation. Last edited December 6, 2021, 06:18. en.wikipedia.org/wiki/Battle_of_Adwa.

"Wikipedia: British Forces Aden." Wikimedia Foundation. Last edited November 13, 2021, 14:42. en.wikipedia.org/wiki/British_Forces_Aden.

"Wikipedia: Derg." Wikimedia Foundation. Last edited December 26, 2021, 14:00. en.wikipedia.org/wiki/Derg.

"Wikipedia: East African campaign." Wikimedia Foundation. Last edited November 30, 2021, 18:26 en.wikipedia.org/wiki/East_African_campaign_(World_War_II).

"Wikipedia: Ge'ez." Wikimedia Foundation. Last edited December 1, 2021, 16:37. en.wikipedia.org/wiki/Ge%CA%BDez.

"Wikipedia: Gondor." Wikimedia Foundation. Last edited November 15, 2021, 12:02. en.wikipedia.org/wiki/Gondar.

"Wikipedia: Gurage people." Wikimedia Foundation. Last edited December 1, 2021, 01:59. en.wikipedia.org/wiki/Gurage_people.

"Wikipedia: Gushl." Wikimedia Foundation. Last edited November 28, 2021, 15:26. en.wikipedia.org/wiki/Ghusl.

"Wikipedia: Human Rights Watch." Wikimedia Foundation. Last edited November 13, 2021, 18:23. en.wikipedia.org/wiki/Human_Rights_Watch.

"Wikipedia: Kebur Zabagna." Wikimedia Foundation. Last edited October 7, 2021, 19:52. en.wikipedia.org/wiki/Kebur_Zabagna.

"Wikipedia: Kingdom of Axum." Wikimedia Foundation. Last edited December 1, 2021, 16:17. en.wikipedia.org/wiki/Kingdom_of_Aksum.

"Wikipedia: Lake Tana." Wikimedia Foundation. Last edited July 29, 2021, 15:12. en.wikipedia.org/wiki/Lake_Tana.

"Wikipedia: Mancala." Wikimedia Foundation. Last edited November 12, 2021, 13:35. en.wikipedia.org/wiki/Mancala.

"Wikipedia: Meskel Square." Wikimedia Foundation. Last edited November 25, 2021, 16:02. en.wikipedia.org/wiki/Meskel_Square.

"Wikipedia: Obelisk of Axum." Wikimedia Foundation. Last edited October 30, 2021, 23:12. en.wikipedia.org/wiki/Obelisk_of_Axum.

"Wikipedia: Salat al-Janazah." Wikimedia Foundation. Last edited December 3, 2021, 09:42. en.wikipedia.org/wiki/Salat_al-Janazah.

"Wikipedia: Shewa Robit." Wikimedia Foundation. Last edited December 2, 2021, 07:40. en.wikipedia.org/wiki/Shewa_Robit.

"Wikipedia: Tarawih." Wikimedia Foundation. Last edited November 5, 2021, 19:55. en.wikipedia.org/wiki/Tarawih.

"Wikipedia: Zewditu Hospital." Wikimedia Foundation. Last edited March 9, 2021, 22:18. en.wikipedia.org/wiki/Zewditu_Hospital.

Endnotes

Introduction

[1] North and South Yemen united in May 1990; they are still united today but have been engaged in civil war since 1994.

Major Life Events

[1] Volumes Two (Yemen) and Three (the US and Canada) are both divided into two parts, as I lived in the US between the two periods I lived in North Yemen, and then I moved to Canada.

I

[1] Danzy Senna, *New People*, New York: Penguin Random House, 2017.

[2] It is common for Ethiopian families to hire young girls or boys as servants. Despite being a poor country, Ethiopia's percentage of homeless people is low because any homeless person can have a simple job working as a servant at any house and can secure accommodation. Most people hire servants, paying them little but providing room and board. That is what I find so unique about Ethiopia—the level of generosity and the ability to share what little they have is an admirable quality that Ethiopian people possess.

[3] In Ethiopian tradition, a visit over coffee is the most valued aspect of catching up and connecting socially. It was during those sessions in 2010 when I learned about the whereabouts of my relatives and incidents of my childhood as well as family births, deaths, and other reflections.

[4] To view these and other photographs, visit adelbenharhara.com/gallery.

[5] To view these and other photographs, visit adelbenharhara.com/gallery.

[6] *Tahasas*. The month of the Ethiopian calendar that coincides with December 10-January 8 in the Gregorian calendar. For more information: travelethiopia.eu/content.aspx?c_id=48F7D6C3-7E63-488D-A4C3-FCE92C5EFC7A&lang=en&cat_id=99359B6D-1358-4FE3-84BF-1FB737EDBE50

[7] For more information: bbc.com/news/world-africa-57443424

—and—

officeholidays.com/holidays/ethiopian-new-
year#:~:text=History%20of%20Ethiopian%20New%20Year,five%20or%2
0six%20timekeeping%20days

—and—

timeanddate.com/calendar/coptic-calendar.html

8 *Hamle*: The month of the Ethiopian calendar that coincides with July 8-
August 6 in the Gregorian calendar. For more information:
travelethiopia.eu/content.aspx?c_id=48F7D6C3-7E63-488D-A4C3-
FCE92C5EFC7A&lang=en&cat_id=99359B6D-1358-4FE3-84BF-
1FB737EDBE501

9 Wikipedia; Wikipedia's "Zewditu Hospital" entry; Wikipedia's entry on the
Zewditu Hospital in Addis Ababa, Ethiopia.

10 When a person dies, Western society turns to a funeral home or
crematorium to take care of the body. In the Islamic tradition, it's different.
According to Islam, death marks the end of a Muslim's life on earth and the
beginning of another, leading to the hereafter. The departure from this life
is thus marked by an act of symbolic purification. Family members often
help wash and bury the body within twenty-four hours.

II

1 Arabs and Ethiopians see or judge a man by his religion rather than his
conduct. My father was defined as an Arab because he was one by ancestry.
But he mimicked the British middle class or ex-military man's lifestyle due
to his extended British military service. He was not a white man; nor did he
think of himself as being an Arab. He was neither Christian nor Muslim. He
was a character of his own. People were confused when trying to define
him, so he was not understood or appreciated for who he wholly was.

2 Wikipedia; Wikipedia's "Ād" entry; Wikipedia's entry on members of the
lost tribe, Ād.

3 Subsequent mentions will use the abbreviation: pbuh.

4 The Awash valley is one of the most important paleontological sites in
Africa. It is in this area where the remains of the famous Lucy, one of the
oldest known human ancestors, were found. For more information:
whc.unesco.org/en/list/10/

Endnotes

III

1 Ahmed Shaikh, "Islamic Inheritance: A Guide for American Muslims," *IslamicInheritance.com*, islamicinheritance.com/islamic-inheritance-guide/
2 Ibid.
3 For more information: hornafricainsight.org/post/amhara-demonization-the-enduring-legacy-of-a-malevolent-narrative
4 Wikipedia; Wikipedia's "Shewa Robit" entry; Wikipedia's entry on the Ethiopian town of Shewa Robit.
5 Yemeni-Hadhrami refers to people from the Hadhramaut area of South Yemen.

VI

1 Wikipedia; Wikipedia's "Lake Tana" entry; Wikipedia's entry on Lake Tana in Ethiopia.
2 Ibid.
3 Ibid.
4 Ibid.
5 *Merriam-Webster.com Dictionary*, s.v. "Agaw," accessed November 29, 2021, https://www.merriam-webster.com/dictionary/Agaw
6 ANU Museum of the Jewish People, "The Jewish Community of Ethiopia," The Museum of the Jewish People, 1996, dbs.anumuseum.org.il/skn/en/c6/e195130/Place/Ethiopia
7 Ibid.
8 Ibid.
9 Wikipedia; Wikipedia's "Geʿez" entry; Wikipedia's entry on the Geʿez language.
10 *Torah*: the first part of the Jewish Bible, specifically Genesis, Exodus, Leviticus, Numbers, and Deuteronomy.
11 The Ethiopian Bible has eighty-one books, compared to the Protestant Bible, which has sixty-six. For more information: borkena.com/2016/06/30/ethiopian-bible-is-the-oldest-and-complete-bible-on-earth-ancient-origine/
12 For more information: learnreligions.com/four-important-numbers-in-judaism-3862364 and myjewishlearning.com/article/judaism-numbers/
13 "Truth to Power: The Book of Esther," Ministry Pass, 2021, ministrypass.com/resource/truth-to-power-the-book-of-esther/
14 "Taʿawwudh is an Arabic term used to refer to the phrase: *Aʿudhu billahi minash-shaitanir-rajim* which means *'I seek refuge in Allah from Shaitan, the accursed one.'*" Source: Sabiqoon Blog Space. "What is Taʿawwudh and

Tasmiyah?" alsabiqoon.blogspot.com/2012/12/what-is-taawwudh-and-tasmiyah.html

15 "Taraweeh is derived from the Arabic word meaning 'to rest and relax'. These special prayers involve reading long portions of the Qur'an, as well as performing many rakahs (cycles of movement involved in Islamic prayer)." Source: Wikipedia; Wikipedia's "Tarawih" entry; Wikipedia's entry on the Tarawih prayer.

16 *Salat al-Janazah*: "The Islamic funeral prayer; a part of the Islamic funeral ritual. The prayer is performed in congregation to seek pardon for the deceased and all dead Muslims." Source Wikipedia; Wikipedia's "Salat-al-Janazah" entry; Wikipedia's entry on the Salat-al-Janazah funeral prayer.

17 *Hammurabi Code*: The Hammurabi Code is "one of the earliest extant sets of laws and one of the best-preserved examples of this type of documents from ancient Mesopotamia … It shows rules and punishments if these rules are broken. The punishments could be as little as a fine or as big as sentencing to death. It focuses on theft, agriculture (or shepherding), property damage, women's rights, marriage rights, children's rights, slave rights, murder, death, and injury." Source: 2007 Wikipedia Selection for Schools, "Code of Hammurabi," accessed December 19, 2021, cs.mcgill.ca/~rwest/wikispeedia/wpcd/wp/c/Code_of_Hammurabi.htm

VIII

1 Wikipedia; Wikipedia's "Mancala" entry; Wikipedia's entry on the mancala games.
2 Ibid.
3 Ibid.
4 Ibid.

IX

1 "What Was the Significance of Jesus Washing the Feet of the Disciples?" Got Questions Ministries, accessed December 16, 2021, gotquestions.org/Jesus-washing-feet.html
2 Ethiopians don't sit on the floor to eat as Arabs do. They have either a traditional Ethiopian- or European-style table My aunt had a European style table. "The *mesob* [is] a woven round wicker basket that can sit as high as three or four feet tall. It has a lid, and when you remove it, there's a place in the center for a tray of food. Each diner sits on a small stool, about eight inches high, called a *barchuma*, and everyone then eats from the common tray

of food." Source: Harry Kloman, "Setting the Ethiopian Table, Ethiopian Food: Mesob Across America,
ethiopianfood.wordpress.com/2013/04/01/setting-the-ethiopian-table/
[3] BililaAward.org, "Abebe Bikila,"
bikilaaward.org/about_us/bikila/index.html
[4] Nilsondm, "Abebe Bikila," 5:23-6:04,
youtube.com/watch?v=9FC8ozQtTEk
[5] Ibid, 7:35-7:59.
[6] Ibid, 14:58-15:58.
[7] For more information: "Abebe Bikila wins Marathon barefooted | Epic Olympic Moments - YouTube:" youtube.com/watch?v=w_Nygi01VqI

XI

[1] His original comment included a word that is highly offensive; I have replaced it with "Oromo."

XII

[1] Alemayehu was the name Emebet and Mamecha called me, and so when writing in my journals, I sometimes referred to myself as Alemayehu in the third person, as if I were a news reporter!

[2] I was eleven, Getahun was five, and Meseret was around four.

[3] My uncle had disappeared in 1970, abandoning me without warning, and then again without warning, he showed up at my aunt's house on the Easter weekend of 1973. He reappeared at her house again in 1976. Why? Because he was homeless and broke. He continually squandered everything he earned. In 1973, he stayed about two or three weeks, and when he was preparing to leave, he wanted to take me with him but my aunt forbade him; she told him he couldn't touch me. Standing up to her older brother at that time in Ethiopian culture was a bold move. I was resentful of how he had treated me, so I enjoyed watching Meseret annoy him and sometimes encouraged her to do so.

XIII

[1] Wikipedia; Wikipedia's "Gurage people" entry; Wikipedia's entry on the Gurage people.

2 Hassan and his father sold items from a small kiosk, like a newsstand, and that is where they also slept.

3 As most Ethiopians spoke Italian, I assume this word was a derivation of *lustrascarpe*, the Italian word for *shoeshine*. As with any new things in developing countries, a language is borrowed from the originator and often evolves.

4 *Birr* is the name of Ethiopia's official currency. In the 1970s, two Ethiopian birr were equal to one American dollar.

5 The basic definition of the term *Muwalladin* refers to someone who is of mixed race, specifically a person who has one parent of Arab descent and one non-Arab parent.

XIV

1 For more information: eatright.org/health/lifestyle/culture-and-traditions/ramadan--the-practice-of-fasting

2 *Eid:* Eid al-Fitr, often referred to as simply Eid, is a religious holiday marking the end of Ramadan, the month-long period of dawn-to-dusk fasting. Children are given money or other treats on Eid. For more information: thenationalnews.com/business/money/how-eidiyah-the-tradition-of-giving-cash-to-children-during-eid-has-evolved-1.1020905

3 "How to Celebrate the Ethiopian New Year," Absolute Ethiopia Tours, absoluteethiopia.com/how-to-celebrate-the-ethiopian-new-year/

4 For more information: Lakachew Atinafu, "Ethiopia: Pagumen, Transitional Month Ethiopians Aspire to Reborn in New-Year," *The Ethiopian Herald*, September 10, 2020, allafrica.com/stories/202009100873.html

5 Priests are always men, as women are considered incomplete. Women aren't even allowed to enter some of the religious facilities. During their monthly cycles, women are kept outside the church and have to pray or worship God through fences.

XV

1 The Imperial Palace.

2 *Biy* and *teter* are marble games. Matias and I used to play marble games with others. I was quite a good player, but he was even a bit better. Therefore, we teamed up and went to different neighborhoods to play with other kids. We cleaned them out and sold the marbles for money.

3 The name of the school was Netsanet Chora.

4 He is referring to my involvement in the EPRP: Ethiopian People's Revolutionary Party—the political party established in 1972 that was instrumental in overthrowing the Ethiopian government in 1973.

5 Gashe Mulugeta was another friend of ours.

6 United States Telecommunication Training Institute.

7 San Francisco State University.

8 The Ethiopian Imperial Guard was the most elite regiment at the time. It was dissolved when the country became communist.

9 Wikipedia; Wikipedia's "Kebur Zabagna" entry; Wikipedia's entry on the Kebur Zabagna (honor guard).

XVI

1 Wikipedia; Wikipedia's "1960 Ethiopian Coup d'état attempt" entry; Wikipedia's entry on the 1960 Ethiopian Coup d'état attempt.

2 Maekelawi is a well-known jail in Ethiopia, which was recently shut down and turned into a national museum.

XVII

1 *Human Rights Watch*: A non-governmental organization (NGO) based in New York City. "The group pressures governments, policy makers, companies, and individual human rights abusers to denounce abuse and respect human rights, and the group often works on behalf of refugees, children, migrants, and political prisoners." Source: Wikipedia; Wikipedia's "Human Rights Watch" entry; Wikipedia's entry on the NGO "Human Rights Watch" based in NYC.

XVIII

1 For more information:
winnipegfreepress.com/breakingnews/Winnipeggers-honoured-for-human-rights-work-78230612.html
and
cbc.ca/news/canada/manitoba/refugee-event-winnipeg-amnesty-international-1.4130642

2 For more information:
facebook.com/100003894802167/posts/2081040325369107/?d=n
—and—

youtube.com/watch?v=s0KQsytqrB0&list=PLWWkfIT_ZSBv-
O0RfaqiPegq_xwqMPa_M&index=10

[3] "The Derg ... officially the Provisional Military Administrative Council (PMAC), was the military junta that ruled present-day Ethiopia and Eritrea from 1974 to 1987, when the military leadership formally 'civilianized' the administration but stayed in power until 1991." Source: Wikipedia; Wikipedia's "Derg" entry; Wikipedia's entry on the Derg.

XX

[1] The two types of crime are still acknowledged today, but at that time, the implications were much more intense; you could be jailed simply for thinking extremist or anti-government thoughts.

[2] *Green:* A term used to refer a darker person. Hadhrami never call a Black man *Black*; rather, they use *green* to avoid the negative connotation associated with the word Black.

Glossary

[1] Wikipedia; Wikipedia's "Ād" entry; Wikipedia's entry on members of the lost tribe, Ād.

[2] Wikipedia; Wikipedia's "Agaw peple" entry; Wikipedia's entry on members of the Agaw ethnic group.

[3] Wikipedia; Wikipedia's "Ghusl" entry; Wikipedia's entry on the ritual of Ghusl.

[4] Wikipedia; Wikipedia's "Gondor" entry; Wikipedia's entry on the city of Gondor, Ethiopia.

[5] Wikipedia; Wikipedia's "Lake Tana" entry; Wikipedia's entry on Lake Tana in Ethiopia.

Appendix One

[1] Insight Ethiopia, "Episode 15: Axumite Kingdom: The Rise and Fall of an Empire," youtube/ad-k2nwJGZw

[2] BBC News Africa, "The Rise of Aksum—History of Africa with Zienab Badawi [Episode 5]," youtube.com/watch?v=A4OSEpexs_Q

[3] Ibid.

[4] Wikipedia; Wikipedia's "Obelisk of Axum" entry; Wikipedia's entry on the Obelisk of Axum.

Endnotes

5 Wikipedia; Wikipedia's "Kingdom of Aksum" entry; Wikipedia's entry on the Kingdom of Aksum.

6 For more information: Wikipedia; Wikipedia's "Aksumite-Persian wars" entry; Wikipedia's entry on the Aksumite Persian Wars.

7 Wikipedia; Wikipedia's "Kingdom of Aksum" entry; Wikipedia's entry on the Kingdom of Aksum.

8 BBC News Africa, "The Rise of Aksum—History of Africa with Zienab Badawi [Episode 5]," youtube.com/watch?v=A4OSEpexs_Q

9 Insight Ethiopia, "Episode 15: Axumite Kingdom: The Rise and Fall of an Empire," youtube/ad-k2nwJGZw

10 Wikipedia; Wikipedia's "Ark of the Covenant" entry; Wikipedia's entry on the Ark of the Covenant.

Appendix Two

1 Wikipedia; Wikipedia's "Battle of Adwa" entry; Wikipedia's entry on the Battle of Adwa.

2 Wikipedia; Wikipedia's "East African campaign (World War II)" entry; Wikipedia's entry on the East African campaign in WW II.

3 Wikipedia; Wikipedia's "British Forces Aden" entry; Wikipedia's entry on the British Forces in Aden during WW II.

4 Neil Orpen, *South African Forces World War II: East African and Abyssinian Campaigns*, October 1968, hibiblio.org/hyperwar/UN/SouthAfrica/EAfrica/EAfrica-18.html

5 "Post-Traumatic Stress Disorder (PTSD)," Mayo Clinic, 2021, mayoclinic.org/diseases-conditions/post-traumatic-stress-disorder/symptoms-causes/syc-20355967

6 Angela, "10 Symptoms of PTSD," *Facty Health*. Updated May 21, 2019, facty.com/conditions/ptsd/10-symptoms-of-ptsd/10/

7 Brian Bethune, "Inside Roméo Dallaire's Ongoing Battle with PTSD," MACLEAN'S, October 21, 2016, macleans.ca/culture/books/inside-romeo-dallaires-brutally-revealing-new-memoir/

8 Ibid.

9 Sheryl Ubelacker, "Romeo Dallaire's Memoir Sheds Light on Former Canadian General's Battle with PTSD," CTV NEWS, last updated Friday October 28, 2016, ctvnews.ca/health/romeo-dallaire-memoir-sheds-light-on-former-canadian-general-s-battle-with-ptsd-1.3135585

Appendix Three

[1] Wikipedia; Wikipedia's "Meskel Square" entry; Wikipedia's entry on the Meskel Square.

[2] Ibid.

[3] Ibid.

[4] "Meskel Festival: Finding of the True Cross," WATA, 2021, www.wata-dmc.net/dmc/travel-fit-products/ethiopia/meskel-festival-finding-of-the-true-cross/

[5] Wikipedia; Wikipedia's "Meskel Square" entry; Wikipedia's entry on the Meskel Square.

[6] Ibid.

[7] "Red Terror Martyrs' Memorial Museum," MOMAA | African Modern Online Art Gallery & Lifestyle, 2021, momaa.org/directory/red-terror-martyrs-memorial-museum/

[8] Wikipedia; Wikipedia's "Meskel Square" entry; Wikipedia's entry on the Meskel Square.

CPSIA information can be obtained
at www.ICGtesting.com
Printed in the USA
BVHW080746010622
638580BV00001B/3